BP 188.3 .F3

THE ISLAMIC VIEW OF WOMEN
AND THE FAMILY

THE ISLAMIC VIEW OF WOMEN AND THE FAMILY

By

Muhammad Abdul-Rauf, Ph.D.

Robert Speller & Sons, Publishers, Inc.
New York, New York 10010

ISBN: 0-8315-0156-1

SECOND EDITION 1979

Printed in the United States of America

To My Wife

بِسْمِ اللهِ الرَّحْمَنِ الرَّحِيمِ

In the name of God,
the Merciful, the Compassionate

CONTENTS

Foreword   13
Introductory Notes About Islam   18

I. MEN AND WOMEN ARE EQUAL

Human Equality   21
Sex Equality   22
Prejudices Against Females Violate Islamic Teachings   23
Respectful Treatment of Women Emphasized   24
Summary   28

II. SEX DIFFERENCES AND SEX ROLES

Men and Women are Different but Not Unequal   31
Wisdom and Value of Sex Differences   32
Sex Differences and Personal Responsibilities   33
Religious Exemptions Granted to Women   34
Women's Modesty   34
Women's Modesty and Female Human Rights   35
The Conjugal Sex Roles   36
Equality and Conjugal Responsibilities   37

III. MARRIAGE AND SEX EQUALITY

What is Marriage?   39
Significance of Marriage   40
Marriage Versus Celibacy   43
Marriage and Personal Freedom   45
Woman's Role in Determining Her Own Marriage   50
Virtues to be Sought in Selecting a Spouse   52
Romance and Spouse Selection   53

IV. DOMESTIC ROLES AND SEX EQUALITY

Social Status and Personal Roles   59
Need for Adjustment   59
Domestic Roles, Possible Alternatives   60
The Workable Pattern   62

Features of the Recommended Pattern   64
Reciprocity and Equity   66
Women and External Work   68

V. THE FAMILY AND THE WOMAN'S POSITION

Structure and Function   71
The Nuclear Family Versus the Extended Family   74
Future of the Traditional Family Pattern   78
Internal Family Organization   80
Factors Cementing Family Ties   83
Value of Child Bearing and Rearing   85
Factors of Domestic Instability   87
Adoption of Children   88
Parental Obligations   90
Filial Duties   94
Further Emphasis on the Mother's Right   95
The Muslim Family in its American Setting   97

VI. TOPICS RELATED TO MARRIAGE AND FAMILY

Mixed Marriage   101
Premarital Activities   103
Sex Practices, Agreeable and Disagreeable   106
Sex Education   114
Polygamy   117
Divorce   119
Common-Law Marriage   123
Birth Control   124
Abortion   125

VII. LIBERATION OF WOMEN

Prejudices Against Women   127
What Has Islam Done for Women?   129
Need for Women's Liberation in Modern Times   133
Women's Liberation Movements in Western Society   136
Liberation of the Muslim Woman   140
Islam and the Modern Feminist Movements   148

VIII. THE UNITED NATIONS' REFORMS

Efforts and Documents 155
International Women's Year 156
The World Conference of the International Women's
Year 157
Declaration on the Elimination of Discrimination
Against Women 158
The World Plan of Action 161

Summing Up 166

Epilogue 168

Bibliography 170

FOREWORD

In early times Human Society was organized on the basis of blood grouping. The members of each social unit believed themselves to belong to a common ancestor. Moreover, each group was a closed, self-maintained unit. Its members cooperated in securing the means of their own survival. They worked together, each identifying his own interests with those of his group. Together they defended their honor and sought their sustenance. The group built their own dwellings, spun and wove their own clothes and baked and cooked their own food. The group was so large and so self-sufficient that the individual member, who was a very precious asset to it, could spend all his life span inside the group and fulfill all his basic and recreational needs within it, including his physical, economic and emotional security.

During its long history on earth, human life underwent profound changes in response to the changing modes of its ecology; but until the industrial revolution, the changes came slowly and the social fabric and the people's values and traditions remained basically intact. Thus, the social unit which maintained its wide structural basis remained large enough to be self-sufficient in spite of these changes. Members of the group were not impelled to leave it for their living. On the contrary, it was difficult and even unimaginable to survive outside of it.

The most dramatic changes in society came about as a result of the industrial revolution, the creation of the machine and the steady progress in the fields of science and technology. People were lured by the glowing promises of quick-cash earnings to leave their traditional homes in order to live near their factories or offices. The huge demographic shifts led to urbanization and the creation of large cities in which the individual who had counted preciously in his traditional home became an anonymous figure in an indifferent setting. Thus released from the traditional censure and falling under the urban pressures and stresses, he very often sought diversion in unhealthy sensual practices which gradually led to criminality and violence against society. On the other hand, the amazing scientific successes and conquests over nature by the industrialized man made him deceitful, weakened his religious commitment and diminished his estimation of his cultural heritage. His loyalty shifted to the machine, and his goal centered on power and earthly achievements. Turning his back to the past, he looked for novelties and new discoveries.

Thus the industrial revolution, which is characterized by mobility, fast movement and rapid changes, has produced fresh ideas and daring philosophies and has led to new modes of behavior. New ideologies were welcomed as invigorating signs of progress, and old taboos and established values were regarded as old-fashioned regression. With greater progress in modern technology in advanced societies, women were relieved from much of the household toil and frequent childbearing, and thus had greater leisure that had to be filled out one way or another. These changes, together with higher age expectation and its attending problems, awakened women to claim their rights and affected the meaning and implications of sex equality.

These rapid and profound changes have given rise to burning questions, leading to the undertaking of useful research projects and the appearance of a rich literature written by social scientists and specialists in all relevant areas, shedding greater light on human nature and promoting greater understanding of the individual and society. Yet, equally large but more widely-distributed literature had been produced, exploiting human weaknesses and low sensual inclinations. Much of this harmful type of literature promotes, at least implicitly, unconventional practices bordering on promiscuity.

These two opposed literary trends dealing as they do with the three interrelated themes: the feminist liberation movement, the so-called sexual revolution, and the institution of marriage, captured my attention since my arrival in America in the mid 1960's. I became increasingly concerned, as I was involved in some serious human situations. Seeing the voice of truth often drowned in the ocean of immodesty and the call for chastity crushed by the torrents of immorality, I felt as if some hidden forces were at work aiming at the elimination of the traditional values which held together the social fabric, through which basic psychological needs were fulfilled and the cherished heritage was successfully transmitted and perpetuated. The traditional patterns of family relationships have been severely disturbed, uncontrolled sensual practices unduly elevated and marriage and its customs abused and condemned. Marriage is sometimes described as the woman's prison and the man's unnecessary burden, and is accused of breeding jealousy and hypocrisy, of perpetuating sexual fascism and of stifling the healthy growth of the individual. Some suggest artificial insemination as a measure of eliminating the need for marriage; some scientists are busy incubating babies in a test tube; and a call is made on people to engage in sex merely for fun. The work of suspected invisible immoral forces is further manifested in widespread pornography. The leniency lent to the promoters of these horrendous practices is much regretted. People talk unrestrainedly of "open marriages", of "swinging couples", of "communal life", of "group sex", of "swapping" and of "homosexuality", as if these appalling practices were natural, moral and healthy pursuits. They read about them, see them illustrated in print, and watch them practiced on the screens and in live shows! Adulterous and incestuous practices are openly confessed and easily tolerated. So much is said of the right of consenting couples, as if their engagement in sexual offenses is as ordinary as sharing a meal or a drink.

I always felt a deep concern, but my hope and my faith in this great country and in the American people never diminished. The public outrage over disclosures of embarassing affairs committed by some leading politicians reveals that under the veneer of permissiveness and tolerated widespread pornography, lies a solid substructure of religious and moral values. Speaking from one's own experience, Americans are basically religiously oriented, God-fearing and charitable. Freedom to them is almost sacred. Yet, we sometimes tend to

forget that every freedom entails equal responsibility. The unbounded love of liberty often impedes the administration of
even those disciplinary measures essential for the correction of
anti-social behavior. In the end, this may prove costly to
everyone.

Church leaders of various denominations have come out
with statements and produced useful literature explaining the
views of their respective churches toward sex, the status of
women, marriage and the institution of the family. This
material has been helpful, not only as guidelines for members
of the church, but also as enlightening sources on crucial
issues for the interested general reader and the student of
humanities. Yet, while the views of the synagogue and the
church over these important issues are readily available, those
of the Mosque, or rather of Islam, the sister faith of Judaism
and Christianity, are hardly accessible. I felt that there was a
need to fill this gap. My reluctance at first was soon overcome
by my feeling that this attempt, if successful, would be a
modest contribution to this great country in acknowledgement
of its generosity in opening its welcoming arms to thousands
of my fellow Muslims who have decided to make it their
home, granting them not only security and a share in its
prosperity but also full liberty to practice the tenets of their
religion.

I was also stimulated, in writing this treatise, by the great
events which have taken place in recent times under the
auspices of the United Nations, related to the objective of
promoting the cause of women's liberation. The World
Organization which is deeply committed to the objective of
improving the status of women throughout the world proclaimed the year 1975, as The International Women's Year.
During that year, conferences on women's rights were convened, proclamations were issued, and recommendations were
made. These events kindled my passion and put me to work
on this book.

One quarter of the world population, mainly concentrated
in developing countries in Asia and Africa, with small
minorities in European countries and the Americas, adhere to
the religion of Islam which espouses a permeating legal system

whereby the faithful are inspired and guided in all situations. In their response to the call for reforms in the area of the status of women, under the pressure of the UN and the stimulation of new ideas and modern trends, the Islamic countries have to react to the dictates of their faith. As a student of Islam who has lived for many years in the West, I felt that there was a need for a statement that would examine the position of Islam vis-a-vis the reforms called for.

Apart from the above factors, I have been motivated in preparing this work by my concern for the well being of my fellow believers living in Western society, particularly those in the Americas. Estimates of their number varies, but it is believed that at least two million Muslims now permanently live in the Western Hemisphere. Their number is increasing daily through immigration and conversion. These people are enduring a transitional stage of conflicts of values: the values they have carried with them from their homeland or have learned from their adopted religion, on the one hand, and the pressure of practices existing in their new society, on the other hand. Hopefully, they will find in the following pages some guiding light that will help in their efforts to steer on a safe course in the land of their choice without compromising the principles of their faith.

December 1976

INTRODUCTORY NOTES
ABOUT ISLAM

Since the views presented in this book are based on the teachings of Islam, it may not be out of place to say a few words here about that religion which, I am happy to note, is now getting an attentive ear in the West after ages of prejudicial misunderstandings. Islam is based upon a firm belief in the existence, perfection, uniqueness and unity of God, Who, in the past, sent Prophets at intervals with missions which contained the seeds of the moral guidance. The noble series of Prophets began with Adam and continued through Noah, Abraham, Moses, Jesus, and many others between them. The divine missions culminated in the ministry of the Prophet Muhammad of Mecca, who, in 610 A.D., when he became forty, began to receive revelations enunciated in words, called *The Koran*. The revelation of these holy words was completed before his death in 632 A.D. The Koran, believed to be the word of God, was written first during the lifetime of Muhammad on his own order. It was also trusted to memory by thousands of his contemporary followers and by succeeding generations, and multiple copies of it were produced and distributed to help in memorizing the words and in checking on the memories.

Followers of Islam, called *Muslims,* firmly believe in all the past Prophets who preceded Muhammad and in their sacred books, especially the Torah, the Psalms and the Holy Gospel of Jesus Whom they love deeply and Whose Virgin Mother they maintain in highest esteem. They believe that their own Book, *The Koran*, as unfolded and interpreted by the words and practice of their Prophet, known as *Hadith*, or *Traditions*, contains the final teachings of God.

Based upon the Koranic and Hadith injunctions and

18

generalizations pertaining to human conduct, a legal spectrum, known as the *shari'ah* or *Islamic law* was immediately developed. As a term, Islamic law may be defined as: "an infallible doctrine regulating the individual's relationship to God and his interactions with his fellow human beings." It comprises the whole of the spiritual, political, economic, social, domestic and private life of the adherents of Islam. Though infallible, the law is by no means rigid. The fact that it is based on principles with relatively few specific injunctions, and that much is left to the judgment of the human mind has made the law reasonably flexible and responsive to the needs of time and environment. Therefore, Islam, which spread within a few decades of its birth into almost all parts of the then known continents and the number of the adherents of which steadily increased—now nearly eight hundred millions, centered in Asia and Africa—was capable of promoting a healthy and stable social order. Under that order, the barriers separating ancient civilizations were demolished. On the enlightened foundations of Islam, blended with remnants of the ancient heritages, a progressive splendid civilization—one of the best history has ever known—was built. Although based on divine revelations, the Islamic law is not a theocratic law, as the faith does not recognize a religious rank. All are equal and have direct access to God. Nor can the law be described as secular, since there is no dichotomy of secular and spiritual in Islam. Apart from the court and its agencies, the sanction of the law is the individual's awareness of God's presence and his desire to be worthy of His pleasure.

In spite of the rise of rival dynasties over the centuries, the unity of the world of Islam was maintained under the operation of Islamic law. The bulk of the Muslim public was oblivious to the political upheavals at the top, and traffic between all parts of the Muslim world continued unhindered throughout the history of Islam. The Arabic tongue was universally used; and the institution of the mosque and its dependancies where travellers found ready hospitality, as well as the professional guilds and the Sufi orders played their roles in maintaining a close Muslim unity. Only when the world of Islam was fragmented under the European colonial rule in recent centuries, and the imposition of foreign legal systems on Muslim lands and the severe pressure of imported values, did the importance of Islamic law diminish along with other unifying factors. Luckily however, the part of the law known as the law of "personal status", dealing with marriage, family and succession, successfully resisted foreign pressure. And now, with the restoration of the Muslim political sovereignty, Islamic law, covering all areas, is gradually gaining firm grounds.

As stated earlier, the views given in this book are based on the law of Islam which is derived from the guidelines found in the Koran and the records of the words and practices traced to the Prophet Muhammad. In other words, this book is not based on the results of interviews of people or laboratory researches, which, in our opinion, are fallible and cannot be a reliable source of guidelines to human behavior. Moreover, social trends are not symptoms of moral ideals, and people's opinions are based on imperfect knowledge and limited experiences. Ideals and infallible judgements can be sought only from the divine guidance deposited in the words of God Who truly knows what is best for all. Nor did we resort to evolutionary interpretations or to social forces said to have been at work in Arabia at the time of the rise of Islam. No such guesses or conjectures are called for, since the Koran started a revolutionary process which immediately altered the old social order and has been actively and efficiently guiding the faithful, especially in the area of family life and related matters. The Koran brought about a social order which was instantly accepted and complied with, and which has dominated the Muslim world until this day.

CHAPTER I

MEN AND WOMEN ARE EQUAL

(a) Human Equality:

> "O mankind, We created you all from a male and
> female, and made you into races and tribes, that you may
> know one another. Surely the noblest among you in the
> sight of God is the most God-fearing of you."
> KORAN XLIX, 13[1]

> "All people are equal, as equal as the teeth of a comb.
> There is no claim of merit of an Arab over a non-Arab,
> or of a white over a black person, or of a male over a
> female. Only God-fearing people merit a preference
> with God." Hadith[2]

The above two texts, a Koranic verse and a well-known
hadith pronounced by the Prophet Muhammad, convey the
principle of universal equality between all mankind in a
strikingly vivid style. Here all divisive factors of race, color,
sex and class are wiped out. It is also important that the principle of equality was immediately put to practice. The people
of Mecca, among whom the Islamic faith emerged, rejected it
vehemently for many years as they were opposed to its egali-
tarian teaching. They used to argue with the Prophet saying,
"How can you claim that our women and slaves and serfs

---

[1] References to Koranic chapters and verses in this work follow the
widely-used Egyptian edition. The *Hadith* references in the coming notes are
to early compilations made by universally recognized authorities. The trans-
lation into English is my own.

[2] Ahmad Ibn Hanbal, *al-Musnad,* Cairo 1930, vol. VI, P. 411. See also
Abd Allah Ibn Abd al-Rahman, better known as al-Darimi; *al-Musnad.*

are of the same standing as ours!"[3]   Much more could be said in this respect, but let us now focus attention on the question of equality of men and women.

(b) Sex Equality:

"To men there is a share of what parents and kinsmen leave; likewise to women there is a share of what parents and kinsmen leave; whether the property be small or large—a determinate share." Koran IV, 7

"To men there is a right in what they have earned, likewise to women there is a right in what they have earned." Koran IV, 32

"And their Lord answered them: Verily I will never cause to be lost the labor of any of you, *be you a male or a female*—the one of you is as the other." KORAN III, 195

"Whosoever of you, *be it male or female,* does a righteous deed, and has faith, We shall assuredly give him (or her) a goodly life, and We shall recompense them their wage, according to the best of their deeds." KORAN XVI, 97

"And the believing men and the believing women owe loyalty to one another, they enjoin noble deeds and forbid dishonor, they perform the prayer, and pay the alms, and obey God and His Messenger. On them will God have mercy; God is All-mighty and All-wise." KORAN IX, 71

"As to the thief, *male or female*, cut off their hands, as a recompense for what they have earned, and a punishment exemplary from God." KORAN V, 38

"The fornicatress and the fornicator—scourge each one of them a hundred stripes . . ." KORAN XXIV, 2

"Tell the believing men to lower their gaze and guard

---

[3]Alfred Guillaume, *The Life of Muhammad,* Oxford University Press 1955, P. 199ff.

their private parts; that will make for greater purity for
them . . . And tell the believing women to cast down
their eyes and guard their private parts, and not to reveal
their adornment save such as is to appear." KORAN XXIV, 30-31

"The Muslim men and women, the believing men and
women, the devout men and women, the truthful men
and women, the enduring men and women, the humble
men and women, the charitable men and women, the
fasting men and women, the chaste men and women, and
the men and women who engage much in God's praise—
for them God has prepared forgiveness and a great
reward." KORAN XXXIII, 35

Here, the following are asserted:

i) The individual, male or female, has a full right over that
which he or she earns; and each is equally entitled to a right of
inheritance in the estate left behind by a parent or a kin. These
rights are further expanded in other Koranic verses and Hadith
instances, as well as in the legal system which developed and
grew on the basis of these sources. Women's rights to possess
wealth, movable or immovable, and their freedom of action
over these properties were fully recognized in measures equal
to those granted to men. These rights were and continue to be
implemented and exercised without restraints throughout the
centuries of the life of Islam.

ii) Men and women are addressed in the same breath as
equally responsible agents, required to observe the law,
promised good rewards for compliance and warned of punishment on disobedience. An interesting point here is that men
and women are equally urged to be chaste, and both are
commanded to lower their gaze and to maintain their chastity.
Neither party is granted a concession.[4]

(C) Prejudice Against Females Violates Islamic Teaching:

_____

l no such concession is granted to women.

"To God belongs the Kingdom of the heavens and the
earth. He creates what He wills. He gives to whom He
wills females, and He gives to whom He wills males. Or
He couples them, both males and females; and He makes
sterile whom He wills." KORAN XLII, 49-50

"And when one of them (the polytheists) is given the
good tiding of a girl, his face is darkened and he chokes
inwardly. He hides from the sight of people out of the
shameful tiding he has been given (pondering) whether he
shall spare the life of the baby girl in humiliation, or
trample her into the dust. Ah! Evil is their judgment!"
KORAN XVI, 58-59

"And kill not your children . . . " KORAN VI, 151

"And behold when the buried female infant shall be
asked: For what sin she was slain?" KORAN LXXXI, 8-9

In the above texts we are reminded of the fact that individuals
are not born as male or female at random, but God Who
possesses the kingdom of the heavens and the earth is
the One who determines whether a baby should be a male or
a female. Believers, as an act of faith, should accept and be
contented with what they are—male or female. Each has a
noble function to achieve. They also should be thankful to
God when they are blessed with a baby, be it a boy or a girl.
Resentment of having a baby girl was a pre-Islamic sentiment,
leading to either burying it alive or letting it survive to suffer
an oppressed status. This unjust attitude and associated
abominable practices have been effectively stopped by Islam.

(d) Respectful Treatment of Women Emphasized:

"And we have charged man concerning his parents—
his mother bore him in weakness, and his weaning was in
two years!" KORAN XXXI, 14

"And we have charged man that he be kind to his
parents—his mother bore him painfully, and she painfully gave birth to him; his bearing and his weaning are
thirty months . . ." KORAN XLVI, 15

"And your Lord has decreed that you should worship
none but Him, and that you should do good to your
parents." KORAN XVII, 23

". . . and live with (women) honorably. If you are averse
to them, it is possible you may be averse to a thing and
God sets in it much good." KORAN IV, 19

". . . then hold fast to them (women) honorably or set
them free on equitable terms. But do not keep them to
injure them, (or) to take advantage of them. Whoever
does that he injures his own soul . . ." KORAN II, 231

". . . if you do good and practice self-restraint (in treating
women,) God is well-acquainted with all that you do.
You are never able to be fair and just as between women,
even if it is your ardent desire. However, turn not away
(from a wife, without determining whether to keep her or
part with her) so as to leave her (as if she were) hanging
in the air . . ." KORAN IV, 128-9

"Someone asked the Prophet: 'Who deserves my service
most after God?' The Prophet said, 'Your mother.' The
person asked again: 'And who is next?' The Prophet
said, 'Your mother.' The man asked further, 'And who
is next?' The Prophet replied, 'Your mother.' The man
asked once more, 'And who is next?' The Prophet, peace
be upon him, said: 'Your father.' " Hadith[5]

"The best of you is he who is best to his wife." Hadith[6]

"Whoever is blessed with two daughters or is taking
charge of two sisters, and treats them well and patiently,
he and I shall be in Paradise like these . . ," gesturing by
his index and middle fingers. Hadith[7]

"Paradise is under the feet of the mothers." Hadith[8]

---

[5]Muhammad Ibn Yazid, better known as Ibn Majah, *Sunan*, Halabi
Press, Cairo, 1953, vol. II, P. 1207.

[6]*Ibid*, vol. I, P. 636. cf. Muslim Ibn Hajjaj, *Sahih*, Halabi Press, Cairo,
n.d., (2 vols.) vol. II, P. 446/7.

[7]*Ibid*, vol. II, P. 1210.

[8]Abu 'Abd al-Rahman Ahmad Ibn Shu'aib, better known as al-Nasa'i,
Sunan, Misriyya Press, Cairo 1930, vol. VI, P. 11.

In these and many other instances the teaching of good treatment of women is emphasized. Parents, after God, deserve our devoted service, but a mother's right for kind filial treatment is triple that due to the father. Also, daughters and sisters are to be treated with tender love and due care. The Prophet Muhammad used to welcome his female cousins and relatives kindly. He offered them his seat and was always ready to extend them a helpful hand.[9]

The Prophet, who had four daughters whom he loved very deeply, treated them kindly and very tenderly. He carried them around and played with them when they were young. When they married, he continued to take great interest in their well-being. From among them, only Fatimah, the youngest, survived her father. The loss of her elder sisters under his eyes, one after the other, was an agonizing experience for the Prophet. He deeply missed Fatimah when she was wed to her husband and moved away from him. The Prophet soon rented a nearby house and moved the couple in it so that they could be close to him. He used to describe his daughter as: "A part of me; who wrongs her wrongs me and who pleases her pleases me."[10] He visited her frequently; and on his return from journeys he called on her first before going home. He often sent for her and her family to share a meal with him. Whenever she approached, his eyes glowed with joy. He took her in his arms, kissed her warmly and offered her his own seat. The Prophet's granddaughter, Umamah, from his eldest daughter, Zainab, was often seen in his arms or on his lap. Sometimes she jumped over his shoulders even when he was solemnly engaged in prayers. When he was to prostrate in prayers he sat her on the floor, but when he rose, she resumed her "seat" on his shoulders again!

This tender pattern of treating young girls became an ideal model for Muslims; and it is refreshing to read the following poem in which a Muslim woman sang the sweet memory of her young age:

---

[9]The Prophet had no sister or brother. He was the only child of his parents, who both died young. His father died before his birth, and his mother died when he was six.

[10]Ibn Majah, *Sunan*, vol. I, P. 644.

Let me remember	*My sweet time*
Let me remember	*My young days*
A baby or child	*I was just a toy*
The world was smiles	*Everything was joy*
I always laughed	*I was always gay*
I always danced	*And always played*
From the bosom of my mother	*To the lap of my dad*
I was the thing they loved	*Their hope and their heart*
When I shined with good health	*They were all glad*
Or became a little sick	*They all became sad!*

The Prophet also set the model of kind treatment due to wives. No marriage could be happier than his to Khadijah, his first wife with whom he lived for twenty-five years before she died. Her death was a severe tragedy to him, and he always cherished her memory. He continued to send gifts to her relatives and friends, saying "I love her and love those who love her."[11] He also said, "The most perfect women were Mary, mother of Jesus, Asiya, the Pharaoh's wife, and Khadijah."[12]

His next young, intelligent, beautiful and resourceful wife, Aisha, used to suffer from a feeling of bitter jealousy when the Prophet praised his former wife. She once said to him, "She was so old; and God has given you a better one."[13] When she saw how angry he became she never repeated that. But he was also kind and tender with Aisha, who lived with him nine years before she was widowed at the age of eighteen. He played games and competed in running with her. Occasionally she took a teasing advantage of his kindness, but he was always patient and forgiving. Once she was seen by her mother beating him on his chest. When her mother began to reproach her, the Prophet said, "Leave her alone. Wives do worse things to their husbands."[14] And when his father-in-law was once about to punish her for a harsh offense against the

---

[11]Muslim Ibn Hajjaj, *Sahih,* Halabi Press, Cairo, n.d. (2 vols.) vol. II, P. 370/1.

[12]Muslin Ibn Hajjaj, *Ibid,* II, P. 370.

[13]*Ibid.*

[14]Abu Hamid, Muhammad Ibn Muhammad, better known as al-Ghazzali, *Ihya' 'Ulum al-Din,* (Halabi Press, Cairo 1958), vol. II, P. 39-40.

Prophet, he stopped him saying, "You are to make peace, not to hurt her."[15]

This perfect example of good treatment of wives was followed by the early generations who were models of Islamic behavior. It is perhaps sufficient to quote Omar's example, the second Caliph, (successor of the Prophet in ruling over the nascent State of Islam). During his reign (634-644 A.D.) Islam enjoyed its most glorious era and witnessed its greatest expansion. His name then inspired awe and respect in the hearts of kings and emperors. Once a man went to Omar's home to complain of his wife. Before entering, he heard Omar's wife shouting at him and using harsh words, but Omar remained calm. The man was embarassed and returned. Omar, noticing a figure going away and thinking that the man might have come for an important reason, called him back and then asked why he was returning without presenting his case. The man explained that he had come to complain of his wife, but seeing how patient the Caliph himself was, he was embarassed to raise his case! Omar, the just, ascetic ruler, who permitted himself only a modest allowance from the state treasury and therefore could not afford to hire some domestic help, told the complainant: "She serves me. She cooks for me. She manages our home. She rears our children. Is it too much to bear up with her occasional naggings?"[16]

Summary:

And thus is the status of women under the law of Islam. It is a status to which a woman is entitled as a basic right, but of which she had been deprived by ages of social and historical prejudices and injustices until it was restored to her by Islam. Under this just status,

As a mother, a woman is to be treated with filial love and veneration,

As a daughter, she is to be treated with parental love and compassion,

---

[15]*Ibid,* P. 40.
[16]Sayyid al Shabalanji, *Nur al-Absar,* 'Atif Press, Cairo, 1963, P. 64.

As a sister, she is to be treated with devoted love, respect and consideration,

As a wife, she is to be treated with constant concern, unbounded care, deep sympathy and loving passion,

And outside these family ties, just simply as a woman, she is:

An individual worthy of dignity and respect,

An independent human being,

A social person,

A legal person,

A responsible agent,

A free citizen,

A servant of God, and

A talented person, endowed, like a male person, with heart, soul and intellect; and has a fundamental equal right to exercise her abilities in all areas of human activities.

CHAPTER II
SEX DIFFERENCES AND SEX ROLES

Men and Women are Different but not Unequal:

Although men and women are equal, they are somewhat different.

In making this statement we do not need to draw on subtle scientific findings, but on tangible concrete factors and easily observable realities. Nor do we invoke such psychological theories as the Freudian claim of a female penile envy on the basis of which he suggests that passivity, masochism and narcissism are basic female features. We reject all of these conjectures which are based on partial clinical observations and are no more than far-fetched guesswork. Such views perpetuate an unfair doctrine of female inferiority.

To an ordinary observer, men and women share common basic biological and mental ingredients which justify and call for their legal, moral and economic equality. Yet there are obviously some somatic differences between men and women, affecting their temperaments, and consequently call in some situations for different but reciprocal sex roles.

Men and women are born with different reproductive systems and some different physiological functions, entailing some psychological and intellectual differences. Men usually have larger bodies, protruding bones, harsher voices and far more hairy faces and bodies. Women have softer skin, larger breasts, gentle voices and good-looking faces. Men ejaculate and women menstruate. Men inseminate and women conceive and lactate. Subtler differences have also been found between boys and girls in certain special abilities and skills. Whether such differences have or do not have a genetic basis, girls are found to become more verbal at eleven, whereas boys at twelve and thirteen are said to do better in mathematics. Girls are also more skillful in patient, minute handwork.

Along with these differences goes a set of psychological differences. While man tends to rationalize, women are said to be more intuitive. Man is harsher and a down-to-earth thinker, and woman is more gentle and sentimental. Man usually has more resistance to emotional provocations, while woman is more sympathetic and tender.

Wisdom and Value of Sex Differences:

This is the way God has created us, for a good purpose; and we have to accept it and submit ourselves to it. The Koran reads:

"It is He Who has created you (all) from one single
soul: and of like nature He created his spouse in order
that he may enjoy comfort in her company." KORAN VII, 189

"And one of His signs is that He has created for you,
from your own type, spouses so that you may enjoy
comfort in their company; and He has made between you
mutual love and sympathy. Verily in this there are signs
for those who reflect." KORAN XXX, 21

". . . Thus is the way God has created the people.
There is no way to change the pattern of God's creation.
This is the best and most perfect way, even though
most people do not know." KORAN XXX, 30

To resent, or to rebel against the way in which we have been created, or to behave in such a way as to manifest this rebellion, is severely condemned. The Prophet, peace and blessings be upon him, is reported to have said:

"Cursed are the men who behave effeminately; and
cursed are the women who behave in a masculine
manner."[1]

[1]Muhammad Ibn Ismail, better known as al-Bukhari, *Sahih,* Halabi Press, Cairo 1953, vol. IV, P. 24.

It is in this way, in which men and women are functionally created different, that each complements the other. Man needs the emotional sensitivity and gentleness of the woman and she needs his masculine matter-of-fact, manly firm shelter. And the child needs his mother's sentimental warm breast and his father's unfailing protection. This is probably part of God's wisdom in creating us so different. However, as Muslims, we accept willingly the way in which we have been created merely because it is God's will and God's action; and there is nothing more pleasing or more deeply inspiring than that which can be derived from the attitude of submission to God's will. This is neither fatalism nor Calvinism, but God's wisdom is far greater than our intelligence. Moreover, the history of mankind tells us that the differences of men and women were always more conspicuous and more emphasized during the splendor of society. In other words, to recognize their differences is more akin to human progress and civilization.

Sex Differences and Personal Responsibilities:

The fact that men and women are so different does not mean that they cannot undertake common tasks or shoulder similar responsibilities. A woman, as an independent responsible agent—a reality fully recognized by Islam—is entitled to work, to trade, to teach, to preach and fill out jobs for which she is as suitably qualified as men.[2] She is also entitled to the fruit of her labor and to equal rewards for tasks she carries out in the same way as men. Discrimination against women is unjust and is therefore forbidden. As a responsible person, a woman is also under the obligation to observe the same religious duties as any man. She is promised the same rewards for compliance and warned of the same punishment on violation, as already observed.

Yet, sex differences are reflected in certain areas; namely, in granting women some religious concessions in certain situations, in laying greater emphasis on feminine modesty, and in the most crucial question of the pattern of conjugal relationship.

---

[2]The controversy over whether women can be ordained does not arise in the Islamic context, as there is no ordination or religious ranks in Islam.

Religious Exemptions Granted to Women:

In the area of religious ordinances, a woman is granted certain exemptions during her periods of menstruation and of birth confinement. During these periods, the obligation of performing the daily mandatory prayers is lifted as a measure of alleviation, not as a manifestation of degradation. If the period falls within the fasting month, the woman is to postpone the obligation of fasting. The same concession is granted during the time of advanced pregnancy.

Allowances and religious exemptions granted to a woman by God during the period of her confinement and heavy pregnancy make her the more entitled for greater consideration by society and, in modern times, for a special confinement leave of absence if she is a working woman. Legislation assuring the right of leave of absence for a confined woman, and even for her husband if need may be, will be congruent with the spirit of the law of Islam.

Women's Modesty:

Another area in which sexual differences are reflected is the greater emphasis on feminine modesty. Women are urged not to reveal their ornamentation unnecessarily in public. The Koran reads:

> "And let them (women) not display their beauty and
> ornaments except what (must ordinarily) appear thereof.
> And let them draw their garment over their bosoms and
> not display their beauty except in the presence of their
> husbands, or their own fathers, or their husbands'
> fathers, or their own sons, or their husbands' sons, or
> their own brothers, or their brothers' sons, or their
> sisters' sons . . . " KORAN XXIV, 31

Now the question is: What is the part of the woman's beauty which is allowed to be left uncovered in public, hinted at in the text? This depends on the context and the need. It depends on whether a woman is giving evidence in court, or undertaking business in the market or studying at school or engaged in laboratory work or working in a factory. The face and hand-palms are commonly interpreted as the parts that can be revealed, but if her duty may require her arms to be uncovered, then this is also permitted. She has to always cover the sensual parts of the body, and to behave decently and with dignity.

This I believe to be the way in which a woman should behave. To do otherwise is to sink below the female dignity and is inconsistent with the woman's claim for equality. Advantage should not be taken of the woman's body and her flesh should not be put on public display. The institutions of hot pants, miniskirts and topless girls are destructive Satanic work. Nowadays, serious thinkers and concerned citizens are worriedly busy resisting legislation allowing easy abortions and those granting marriage licenses to couples of the same sex. Yet, we have ourselves to blame! When a section of the moral edifice is allowed to be broken the whole structure weakens and gives in easily to pressure. And thus tolerance of an evil leads to other evils. First we condone female public exposure; next dating and easy mixing; next, pre-marital "games"; next, extra-marital relations and open marriages; next, the elevation of open homosexuality to an acceptable normal status; and next, uni-sex marriages. Where, and when, shall we stop? How can we profess to be either Christian or Islamic when we openly disobey and disavow our respective scriptures and religious edicts?[3]

The result: Broken laws, blood relations torn apart, deep dissatisfaction, a criminal climate, a disquieting sense of insecurity, fear and mutual mistrust, wide-spread corruption, irresponsible strikes, uncontrolled inflation, more frequent cases of rape, and the threat of depression and bankruptcy.

Woman's Modesty and Female Human Rights:

The emphasis laid on the need for a woman to guard her modesty and not to reveal her attractions publicly is by no

---

[3]Women's modesty has thus its cultural and religious roots. It does not derive, as some psychologists claim, from an envious sense of shame and the woman's desire to cover her castrated wounds.

means inconsistent with her human rights or with her freedom and power over her body. Her decent behavior is the only way which is in keeping with her dignity and right of equality. A woman is a sweet creature, and can easily be seductive. Her gaze can be seductive; so is her voice, her gait, her bosom, her legs and the form of her feet and the shape of her ankles. If you leave a sweet thing uncovered, you will be inviting swarms of dirty creatures to prey upon it and corrupt it. The current wave of rape incidents in regions where public exposure of women prevails, as well as the widening phenomenon of infidelity, strengthens our argument beyond any doubt.

I do question the wisdom of the wide-spread publicity given to statistics of infidelity. This publicity has its adverse effect. It makes it look like something almost normal or agreeable and conduces the weaker souls to yield easily to the temptation. This argument is supported by the worsening conditions since the publication of the Kinsey Report around the middle of this century. While Kinsey in 1953 found 9% of American married women under the age of 25 had indulged in what is euphemistically called an "extra-marital affair", an investigation carried out by Redbook Magazine and published in its issue of October, 1975, has found that the ratio has jumped to 25%. It is even predicted that eventually half of the American wives will engage in this destructive immorality. And so, in covering her body, a woman protects her honor, maintains her dignity, and shields her beauty from corrupting lustful aggressors. Her liberty and human rights are thereby further enhanced.

The Conjugal Sex Roles:

The most complex role situation in which sex differences may have to be reflected is that related to husband-wife relationship, being the most intimate and most personal type of relationship. It is also very closely tied up with the emotional life of the persons involved and has a profound bearing upon the raising of human offsprings. It entails sustained interactions between the spouses and its quality is of crucial concern to them. It is this relationship through which the female makes her noble and fundamental contribution to humanity: the perpetuation of the humankind, and by which she and her husband are provided with devoted, trusted, committed and lasting companionship. It is under the auspices of this relationship that young human beings are nurtured and prepared to face the challenges of an open aggressive world.

Success of spouses and parents in their crucial function depends upon the degree of harmony between their mutual roles within their domestic unit.

The pattern of domestic sex roles, as recommended in Islam, will be discussed at length in a later chapter. To put it here in a nutshell, it may be defined as *a flexible pattern of reciprocal and complementary attitudes to be assumed by the couple, in which the leadership of the domestic team is vested in the husband.* This is a leadership of responsibility, not a leadership of superiority. It is so prescribed in the interest of the domestic team.

Equality and Conjugal Responsibilities:

I strongly believe that the functional complementary pattern of conjugal relationship in which the husband is made legally responsible for the wellbeing and the cost of living of his wife and children is far better and more peacefully workable than an arrangement in which the wife has to share in the financial burden of the household, now being advocated in some quarters on the basis of full equality. This advocated alternative is likely to lead to quarrel between the couple. Yet, there is nothing to prevent the wife from sharing the financial domestic responsibilities on a voluntary, rather than legal, basis. A voluntary contribution, rather than a legal obligation, enhances better conjugal relations. Furthermore, it is our view that a wife is better off when she feels legally free from the financial burden and that she can always depend on a responsible, loving, devoted husband. It is more congruous with her femininity and gives her a greater sense of security. To throw the total legal burden on the husband, on the other hand, harmonizes more with his tougher nature and enhances his sense of manliness and generous responsibility.

The sex role differences, or rather, the unequal domestic responsibilities, implicit in the pattern of conjugal relationship advocated in this work, is by no means inimical to the true concept of human or sex equality. As defined earlier, equality means equal entitlement to human dignity, to respectful treatment, to free choice and freedom of action. It is equality before God and before the law. It is equality of religious and moral responsibility. Domestic sex roles, on the other hand, have to provide certain functional diversities arising from the natural sex differences which are not at all inconsistent with that sense of equality. If the male is a better woodcutter, which is an honorable profession, the woman's child-bearing is an essential and by no means less noble function. Similarly, a housewife's job is not at all less important than her husband's engineering or executive duties. Attaching greater value to one of these reciprocal functions over the other is arbitrary and unjustified. Therefore, sex role differences should not imply a sense of inferiority or superiority to one party over the other.

The operative law in the distribution of duties and functions among the members of a group must take account, in the interest of the total welfare of the group, of the qualities, abilities of, and differences between these members. The sex differences are paramount among these factors. Therefore, the role of a male may have to be different from the role of a woman, depending on the type of the social unit and its needs, as well as the status of the individual in this unit. When the sex of the individual has nothing to do with his status and function in the group, then the female and male roles can be similar. A school master and a school mistress, for instance, may have the same status and the same roles and therefore should have the same reward. Many similar examples can be quoted, but a husband and wife in a family have a different status each on account of their sex differences. Therefore, their roles have to be different. Here again, the difference in the roles they play in the family, which are equally important but complementary and reciprocal, should not carry with it a value judgment of superiority or inferiority, even when there is a degree of inequality of authority in the interest of the group.

CHAPTER III
MARRIAGE AND SEX EQUALITY

What is Marriage?

Marriage is: "A solemn contractual agreement between an eligible male and an eligible female, concluded in the presence of witnesses, whereby they become acknowledged as husband and wife". A union, short or long, between two persons of the same sex, is not a marriage but an ugly homosexuality. An agreement between a number of men and a number of women to live together sharing communally their sexual services, is not a marriage but immoral and asocial promiscuity. A liaison between a marriageable couple without a duly-witnessed contract is adulterous.

Marriage alternatives, widely talked about in recent years, and becoming features of the so-called "sex revolution"—cohabitation contract, open marriage, swinging couples, swapping, and a variety of some other unhealthy loose morality—cannot be recognized as legitimate life styles. Sex relations through these arrangements are unethical and illegal from our point of view. They are simply adulterous violations. Marriage implies the exclusive right of each mate of the couple to the sexual favors of the other; and its contract has to conform with well-defined prerequisites, which include a vow made by the marrying couple in front of lawful witnesses.

Thus the marriage contract as conceived of by Muslims is a legal commitment sanctioned by God and acknowledged by society. It does not have to be conducted at the hands of a "clergyman", as Islam does not recognize religious ranks. Yet, since the Islamic faith attaches religious values to all types of human behavior, the marriage contract is both a civil agreement and a religious commitment which should be respected and should endure as far as possible.

Talks of marriage alternatives in recent years remind us of the loose practices which prevailed in Arabia before the advent of Islam which came and put them to an end. It is related that four types of marriage were practiced during the pre-Islamic era. One was like our familiar form of marriage. Another type was practiced when a couple desired to have a child of a superior descent. The wife, on the cessation of her monthly menstruation discharges, went to live with a man of nobility until she became pregnant by him and then returned to her former husband. A third type of marriage which was current before Islam allowed a number of men, not more than ten, to enjoy the sexual favors of a woman, one after the other, until she became pregnant. When she gave birth to a child, she sent for all her lovers, and none could decline her invitation. When they gathered together she addressed them, saying: "You all know what has happened and this is the child who belongs to so and so", naming any one of them. The named person could not challenge her claim. He accepted his status as father of the child and became the husband of the woman. In the fourth form of the pre-Islamic marriage, prostitution was involved. Before the advent of Islam, there were many prostitutes and they used to plant a flag in front of their doors. When one of them delivered a child, she invited those with whom she had cohabited, and named one of them as father on the ground of resemblance in the child's features. The man accepted the child and became the husband of its mother.[1] Islam stopped all these ugly practices and breathed a fresh sweet fragrance into the nuptial commitment.

Significance of Marriage:

Reproduction in an organized wholesome manner is admittedly the ultimate objective of the institution of marriage. Yet Islam lays a great emphasis on the almost equally important function of marriage as a means of providing companionship

---

[1]Abu Dawud, *Sunan,* vol. II, P. 249.

and a measure of fulfilling certain other fundamental needs.

The Koran, in speaking of this basic function of marriage, draws attention to the divine wisdom in creating mankind as a bisexual species, reproduced through mating between two members of the same species but of different sex. It reads:

"And one of His signs is that He created for you, of
your species, spouses that you may repose in them; and
He has set between you love and mercy. Verily in this
there are signs for a people who reflect." **KORAN XXX, 21**

Here mankind is stated to be created as a biocious (bisexual) being; reproduced through mating of two genetically similar parties, one to fertilize and the other to conceive.

God could have created mankind as a monocious (monosexual) being, reproduced naturally without need for mating or in such a way as to reproduce through mating with a member of another species. Yet, God has chosen to create man as a biocious being, reproduced through mating with members of his own species. The Koran states that the purpose of creating man in this biocious pattern is to let each mate provide comfort, companionship and a feeling of true care and concern for the other. Such comfort, companionship and a feeling of mutual care and concern could not be afforded in the absence of easy communication. Between two communicating members of humanity, there can be reactions and interactions and cooperation and mutual understanding. These actions, reactions and interactions lead to fulfillment of the mental and psychological needs of the mating couples. And when they are committed believers, they realize that their love of each other is derived from their commitment and loyalty to God. Each sees in serving the other a service to God and obedience to Him. Their mutual love is therefore more durable and heavenly. Even in their act of love they feel a deeper and more enduring joy, resembling their anticipated delight in Paradise when they are closer to their Creator.

On the other hand, marriage is essential for one's personal fulfillment. It complies with the divine scheme of the universe, of which the individual is a tiny but meaningful part with a significant mission to achieve. By fulfilling his mission, he fulfills himself and his legitimate needs, including his longing for recognition and for a warm sense of being wanted.

The Koran reads:

"And I have only created the *jinnis* and mankind in order that they may serve Me." KORAN LI, 56

And the Prophet relates on behalf of God:

"I was a hidden treasure and longed to be known. So, I have created the world so that I may be known."[2]

God the Almighty created the universe and everything in it. He made man the best of His creations, endowing him with psychological, mental and spiritual faculties not given to the other creatures. In fact, the human features are endowed, *first*, in order that man may achieve the purpose of the whole creation: namely, to serve God and fulfill His Will. The complex makeup of man makes him yearn for the pleasure of his Creator, and makes him also capable of doing whatever may bring him closer to this end. So, man is the ultimate purpose of the creation of all other things, which are actually created for the sake of man and for his service and use. In turn man is so created to serve God and fulfill His Divine Will.

For man to serve God and fulfill His Divine Will, man must always observe God in all his movements and in all his thoughts and obey the laws and the rules of his Creator. Some people may erroneously think that God is served merely by observing religious ritual duties, such as the performance of prayers, fasting and by doing similar things. But these activities constitute only one area of serving God. He is to be served also in all other types of human activities, simple or complex, pleasurable or painful, individual or social, physical or intellectual. That is what we mean when we say that Islam encompasses all aspects of human life, even including the manner of eating, the manner of walking and the manner of talking. It teaches us to walk gracefully and respectably and to

---

[2]Abu al-Su'ud, *Tafsir*, Cairo, 1928, P. 634.

talk politely and to dress decently.[3] It urges its adherents to do anything and everything that would promote peace and mutual love; to greet each other and to pay visits to one another.[4] It prescribes hard work and encourages the study of the natural forces in order to harness them for the service of man.[5] So long as the individual undertakes his activities, whether in serious or recreational areas, intending to obey thereby God's laws and to integrate himself as well as he can in the universal scheme, even though he may also be serving himself, he is promoting better relationship with his Lord and is making himself more worthy of the Divine pleasure and the Divine rewards both in this world and in the Hereafter.

Marriage Versus Celibacy:

Under the Islamic law, it is undesirable for a marriageable person to remain single, even when the intention is to be free to concentrate on prayers and on similar religious ordinances. The "monastic" attitude has no place in Islam, as declared by the Prophet.[6] Once he heard some of his companions talking of their intention to fast every day, to stay up for worship all the night long, and keep away from the company of women. He criticized that attitude and urged moderation, adding:

> "I myself fast some days and do not fast some other days. I sleep part of the night, and stay up (in worship) the other part of the night. And I enjoy women through marriage."[7]

'Amr, a renowned Muslim general, conveyed to the Prophet a complaint from his daughter-in-law against his own son, Abdallah. The latter had abandoned his wife at night and did not share her meals during the daytime. Throughout the night time young Abdallah was engaged in prayers and Koranic

---

[3]*The Koran,* XXXI, 18/19; XVII, 37 and VII, 31/32.
[4]*The Koran,* LXII, 37-43; IX, 6-13; IV, 86 and XXIV, 27-29.
[5]*The Koran,* IX, 105; VII, 85; and XVI, 4-18.
[6]Muslim, *Sahih,* vol. I, p. 584. Cf. Ibn Majah, *Sunan,* vol. I, p. 593.
[7]Abu'Abd al-Rahman, Ahmad Ibn Shu'aib, better known as al-Nasa'i, *Sunan,* Misriyya Press, Cairo 1930, vol. VI, p. 60.

recitation, and during the daytime he was always fasting. The Prophet summoned Abdallah, advised him of moderation and told him:

> "You may fast some days but do not fast the other days. Stay up (in worship) part of the night, but sleep and rest the other part of the night. Your body has a right upon you. And your wife has a right upon you."[8]

Men and women are urged to get married early; and fear of poverty should not be a discouraging factor. The Koran assures that God shall provide for them from His unbounded favors. (KORAN XXIV, 32)

Marriage, admittedly, may have disadvantages. It is a burden and added responsibilities; and when it is unsuccessful, it is a hell. Yet, there is no rose without some thorns. Its merits far exceed its evils. And a careful search for a compatible spouse should make marriage failure an exceptional phenomenon. After all, our adventures in life are hardly free from the element of risks. Marriage casualties should not deter us. Take the wise steps, and leave the result to God.

Celibacy, on the other hand, is boredom, lonesomeness, and a deprivation. In a recent study, an author has found out that married Americans were far happier and more satisfied than singles.[9] Another author asserts that marriage is the crucial institution of civilized life, having found that men who do not marry make less money, commit more crimes, take more drugs, and get more crabs, herpes, simple and venereal diseases than married men.[10] Also, Ann Landers in her column states: "According to my medical friends and experts in the field of mental health, married men fare much better than bachelors. Bachelors have more physical illnesses and more emotional breakdowns. They drink more and have shorter life spans. They are seven times more likely to commit crimes and twenty-

---

[8]Muslim, *op. cit.,* pp. 469/70.

[9]Angus Campbell, "The American Way of Mating, Marriage Si, Children Only Maybe," *Psychology Today,* (May, 1975), based on a survey of 2,164 adults.

[10]George Guilder, *Naked Nomads: Unmarried Men in America,* (Quadrangle), 1974, p. 8ff.

two times more likely to be in prison or jail. Every happiness poll I have ever read indicates that single men are the unhappiest lot in the world."[11]

Apart from the above factors, I do not deem it reasonable to support an attitude in life that would, if universalized, endanger the interests of humanity. To discourage marriage and advocate widespread celibacy as an alternative lifestyle, if the call is heeded, would threaten the well-being of the human race. If our aim of life is the pursuit of happiness, both on earth and in the Hereafter, marriage is certainly a means that provides delightful companionship and also is a religious practice that pleases our Lord and makes us worthy of His rewards.

Marriage and Personal Freedom.

The wide publicity on sexual misconduct in recent years has led to a trend of increasing permissiveness, to undue disregard to traditional moral values and to widespread pornography. Certain forces exploited the circumstances to their own advantages, playing on the lower instincts of man. Revolt against the traditional heritage has been manifested in recent years in anarchic lifestyles and severe attacks on marriage, which has been accused of being the woman's prison and the millstone around man's neck.

Absurd "arangements" are forged as substitutes to the wholesome traditional marriage in which a man and woman live together in bliss, happiness and chastity. They talk of such things as open marriage and swinging couples. Literature suggestive of sinister immorality with no respect for conjugal relations or moral virtues is produced in abundance. One feels as if man, in his quest for orgasm and excitement, descends to the indignity of a lower animal—and even worse. Satisfaction

---

[11]Ann Lander's Column, *The Washington Post,* June 17, 1975. The fact that single women have fewer suicides and psychological disorders than married women, as asserted by Professor Gore of Vanderbilt University is not inconsistent with this argument, and should not be attributed to marriage itself but to exaggerated unfulfilled anticipations, infidelity and shallow or no religious commitment.

of the sexual urge is legitimate and important; but it should not unreasonably occupy too much of our time and attention. Our forefathers achieved full satisfaction in that area without all that extravagant degree of preoccupation. They did not need the preaching of a Freud, or the counsel of Masters and Johnson. They were even much happier and better adjusted. From their literature, they appear to have achieved the greatly sought-for multiple orgasm without modern counselling.

One feels uncomfortable when reading such misleading attacks against the institution of marriage. Some writers regrettably take undue pride in retaining their single status, singing their liberty to eat when they want, to sleep when they want, to read when they want and to write when they feel a desire to do so—unrestrained by the chains of marriage. An authoress curried her thoughts with the tales of her exploitation of the male friends who, one after another, fell into her arms and then she cast them over when she had gotten all she wanted to get out of them! Another emphasizes her point in these words:

> "A lover who comes to your bed of his own accord is
> more likely to sleep with his arms around you all night
> than a lover who has nowhere else to sleep."[12]

Do my readers agree that marriage imposes so much restraint on the spouses, as implicit in such writing? Can we all live a completely unfettered life without threatening the survival of mankind? Being human, intelligent and responsible, we should be prepared to accept a degree of restraint and sacrifice. The individual liberty ends when the freedom of the others is threatened.

If I may digress a little here, I should like to say that reading such views advocating unbounded freedom reminds me of my childhood dreams and innocent thoughts when I used to go out of the village in which I was born and reared, into the open fields to enjoy the cool fresh breeze under the trees.

I used to look up at the dancing branches and the shivering leaves at the top of the trees, envying the singing, jumping lit-

---

[12]Germaine Greer, *The Female Eunuch,* (McGraw Hill, 1971), page 242.

tle birds, picking the fruits which my little hands could not reach. I used to ponder for long sessions over the liberty enjoyed by these little birds, and wish I were one of them, flying at will in the expanse of space, crossing rivers, surveying mountain tops, moving from orchard to orchard, choosing the best of the fruits, and returning at dusk to rest in my warm nest.

I used to sit and touch and smell the green grass and the beautiful flowers, and gently wipe the drops of the morning dew from their tiny leaves, wishing I were myself a flower or a piece of grass, left alone to grow so freshly in the open air, unthreatened by the cane of my Koranic school teacher and undisturbed by the fear of his painful displeasure whenever I committed an error.

I used to look up and watch these little birds and tenderly touch the flowers and the grass, lamenting my hard fortune, recalling the heavy steps I had to walk early in the morning every weekday to the Koranic school, repeating the prescribed portions of the text I had to learn at home to recite from memory unto my teacher, without an error. I remembered the scars which I sustained from my teacher's cane, and the protest of my loving mother but to the pleasure of my father who saw them as blessings and a good omen of my future success. He had vowed to assign his first-born son to the pursuit of religious learning. In preparation for admission, I had to learn, in the hard way, all our Holy Book by heart, scared in the oppressive climate of the Koranic school, and escaping in daydreams and fantasies.

Once, while my mind was innocently floating over these fantasies, envying these birds and the freely-dancing flowers and leaves, the flow of my thoughts was interrupted by a sudden noise of the frightened birds flying away, and a thud on the ground under a tree. I turned, and saw a fierce-looking boy running to pick up a poor little bird which he had shot with a stone, and had dropped with a bleeding wing! I felt a stab piercing my heart which began to flutter; and a burning fire in my eyes which started to flow with tears. Still suffering the painful thoughts brooding over the misfortune of the poor little bird, I was further dismayed by the sound of a buffalo crushing the flowers under her large, clumsy feet and mercilessly cutting and chewing the grass with her sharp thoughtless teeth.

I then reflected further: Would I like to be a bird exposed to the misfortunes of that little bird? Or to be a flower or a grass that could be so easily crushed and chewed? I was then very disheartened; and was thus awakened to the irresistible reality that there could be no unrestrained happiness or unchecked liberty.

* * * * *

When I read such material attacking the institution of marriage for the sensible restraint it entails, the train of innocent thoughts of my childhood come back to mind and I feel as if those writers were living in a world of dreams from which they would one day be awakened to the realities of their lonesome life. Marriage affords a committed companionship which provides, when successful, infinite sensations of shared happiness that cannot be experienced in a non-responsible, spiritless and mainly sensual short-lived relationship. A wife at home is not a bird in a cage. She is a bird in a warm nest, wooing her mate and tending her chicks lovingly, eagerly and very happily.

Love of liberty is deeply embedded in the hearts of all human beings, and especially the American people. Historical and environmental factors reinforce and perpetuate American democracy. Yet, undue advantage seems to have been and to be still being taken of the American tolerance by certain elements inimical to the cherished moral heritage. They seek to redefine essential concepts such as maleness, feminineness, love and commitment, in such a way as to corrupt the people's conscience and eliminate its repulsion to perversive practices.

Emphasis has shifted from regard for divine teaching and obedience to conscientious dictates in determining the quality of human interactions, to merely mutual consent of the parties concerned. The release from focus on divine guidance, which did not only play an effective role in maintaining efficient social order in the past but also fed the human soul with comfort and contentment, has led to unspeakable confusion, anarchical morality, despair and widespread psychological disorders.

In the area of sex, chastity is regarded as old-fashioned puritanism; loose conduct is portrayed as a manifestation of freedom and progress; and love-making between unmarried but consenting couples is no longer blameworthy. Yet a victim of rape under compulsion, if she ventures to report it, has to sustain severe injuries in her struggle against the aggressor in order to prove that she was compelled! In the confusion, her resistance is occasionally misinterpreted as consent, and use of deceptive claims to lure her to surrender is not deemed as a measure of coercion.[13]

Under such circumstances, countless numbers of sexual criminals are set at large, while their victims are left to suffer all the severe consequences. So long as they are not restrained by conscience or the fear of the Lord, and can escape the attention of the court or get out of it easily, they are even encouraged to continue their criminal pursuit and violence against society.

Provocative literature is produced in abundance nowadays in the form of fiction and non-fiction. Some caters to singles, some to male homosexuals, some to lesbians. Some speaks of the sensual man, some of the sensual woman, and another of the sensual couple. Noble restraint is painted as a reactionary conduct based on traditional illusions, and perversions are said to be the cutting edge of a desirable social transformation based upon the "revolutionary" assumption that sexuality need not be subjugated to the demands of procreation, and that people are created with a variety of impulses which should be allowed to be cultivated rather than suppressed!

Moral restraint is not an encroachment on human freedom, but a reasonable sacrifice for the sake of human dignity and in the interest of society and for the pleasure of God. The purpose of human activities is both to benefit the individual and to contribute to the social order. Neither the need of the individual nor that of society should be so stretched as to adversely affect the legitimate purpose of the other. Islam

---

[13]*TIME* Magazine, May 12, 1975, P. 55.

promotes the communal interests above all; yet it respects the individual's needs, sentiments and emotions. It calls for a moderate compromise, involving sensible sacrifices.

Woman's Role in Determining Her Own Marriage:

The crucial steps of the procedural process of marriage are the selection of a spouse and the marriage contract. According to the Islamic law, as we shall see, the role of the bride in these two steps is essential to the validity of the marriage.

The most interested party in selecting a future mate for a person is the person himself or herself, who is to share with the individual to be selected the stresses and pleasures of life.

In the olden days young people did not part on marriage from their kin groups, whether the group was of the patrilocal or matrilocal traditions. In patrilocal societies the marrying boy remained with his group, and his bride moved in and lived with them. In matrilocal societies the girl remained with her clan and her groom joined her. Therefore, the kinsfolk of a person were interested in his or her spouse who was going to live closely with them. Moreover, tribesmen were deeply concerned about the children who would come out of the wedlock of their members. These children were to be important integral assets of the blood group. Kinsfolk were therefore very much interested in the marriage of their members and were deeply involved in making the decision of the selection of their spouses. In some societies, the choice of a spouse for members of the clan was traditionally confined to certain degrees within the tribal ties.

With the growing human mobility and individualism, the circle of interested kin in selecting the spouse of one of their members was narrowed down to one's own parents. Yet, in modern times the parents' right to participate or to dominate in making the choice of a spouse of their child has been severely challenged or even denied, although it still holds in varying degrees in some societies.

Thus, in olden days, the marriageable boy and girl, by virtue of tradition, did not have much to say in picking his or her mate. That was the privilege of the parents, whether they made the choice directly or through a "go-between", or through a "marriage broker". This was the prevailing condition in patriarchal Europe and in societies dominated by the ancient Eastern cultures.

As a result of industrialization, urbanization and the greater mobility of population, new styles have emerged in modern society. The individual, boy or girl, is said to have gained "independence" or "freedom". Thus, the boy and girl in the West now freely choose their spouses independently from their parents, no matter how the parents might feel about the choice. This freedom, in addition, must entail experimentation and trial, which in turn require free mixing between the sexes, dating, and premarital activities.

The choice of a spouse, we believe, should be based upon personal virtues of enduring values, and should be the common concern of the young person who is to get married and his or her parents whenever their wisdom and experience may be helpful. The consent of the marrying child, however, should be the determining factor, although the decision should be deliberated and approved by the family. We hardly need to emphasize the advantages of this arrangement, in terms of the durability and success of marriage. This can be easily corroborated by recent statistical data.[14] The acceptance of a parental share in making the selection for the child in this most important area is in line with the filial duties strongly recommended in Islam. The family's role should depend on the context and the conditions of the prevailing social order.

Legally speaking, however, the consent and wishes of the marrying person, boy or girl, is of primary importance. Neither should be married to a person against his or her

---

[14]A report published in *The Evening Star and Daily News* (Washington, DC, November 15, 1972), under the title "Arranged Marriages Likely Fewer Divorces", states: "Studies by the Japanese Government indicate that 'arranged marriages are likely to result in fewer divorces than love marriages' ". The same report states that arranged marriages "account for an estimated 95 percent of marriages in India, about half of those in Japan and South Korea, well over half in Malaysia and three-quarters or perhaps more among the overseas Chinese in Southeast Asia". The same report acknowledges that parental control over their children accounts for the endurance of marriage in India.

wishes. A question only arises in the case of a girl marrying for the first time, who has had no sexual experience, whether the concurrence of her guardian is required. There is a strong tendency in some legal Muslim circles to recommend the advisability of seeking the concurrence of the girl's guardian, especially the father or the father's father in the absence of the former. The intention is to safeguard the interests of the girl, especially when she is marrying for the first time. They say that men are like locked boxes, and an innocent inexperienced girl may become easily infatuated with the wrong man. The mutual decision taken by a father and his daughter in choosing a mate for her, in which the girl's wishes as well as her best interests are taken into consideration, is no doubt the best alternative. However, a father or guardian is forbidden to withhold his consent when a suitable match proposes to his daughter. Under no circumstances should a guardian compel a girl to marry someone against her choice. In the contract of marriage, it is recommended that the bride takes the initiative by offering herself in marriage, to which the groom responds by indicating acceptance of her in marriage. The desirability that the bride takes this initiative emphasizes the fact that she is entering into the marriage contract through her free will. If her guardian represents her in the contract, the person who conducts the ceremony has to see the girl first and make sure that she consents to the marriage. The Prophet is reported to have said:

> "A single girl, not her guardian, is in possession of herself."[15]

Virtues to be Sought in Selecting a Spouse:

Whether the choice of a spouse is made by the marrying child alone or in collaboration with the parents, the greater consideration should be given to the moral character of the person to be picked. An individual of a responsible conscience and good conduct will earn your trust and confidence, and will be a soothing and comfortable companion. Graceful behavior

---

[15]Ibn Majah, *Sunan,* I, 601.

adds greatly to the charms of the person. It would also be better if the one you choose is of an age which approximates yours. This makes communication easier. Physical beauty is certainly a great asset in marriage. A couple contemplating marriage are therefore encouraged to see each other prior to marriage in order to ensure their satisfaction and avoid disappointment. People differ in their taste, and have their personal preferences. Likely fertility is also of great value and should be borne in mind in making the choice. Wealth should not be given too much weight. God changes people's fortunes overnight.

In this context, let us quote the following relevant words of the Prophet, peace and blessings be upon him:

> "A woman may be chosen in marriage for her wealth, or for her beauty, or for her nobility or for her good religious conduct. Pick the one who is morally motivated and hold fast to her."[16]

> "A child-bearing woman lacking in beauty is better than a beautiful but infertile one."[17]

And a wise author says:

> "A desirous woman with wide bright eyes, flowing beautiful hair, a smooth bright skin, who is of good conduct and who loves her husband and is devoted to him, is indeed one of the maidens of Paradise."[18]

Romance and Spouse Selection:

The so-called romantic love has become the major factor in making the choice of spouses these days in the West. The couple is first acquainted; then they date; the relationship blooms and grows steadily in warmth; then experimentation is made with no restriction, involving necking, foreplay, and

---

[16]Al-Bukhari, *Sahih,* vol. III, p. 150. Cf. Ibn Majah, *Sunan,* vol. I, p. 597.
[17]Abu Hamid Al-Ghazzali, *Ihya' 'Ulum al-Din,* Halabi Press, Cairo 1958, vol. II, p. 24.
[18]*Ibid,* p. 36.

even love-making. After a period of varying length, the couple may decide to get married, often after the accident of conception.[19]

This custom is now almost universally acknowledged in the West as normal. The boy and the girl, each, may be also involved in experimentation with other parties before they make up their minds and before each fixes his or her affection on the choice he or she makes. In order to help the young girls guard themselves against unwanted conception, contraceptive materials and instruction in their use are made easily accessible. Mothers teach their daughters how to use them efficiently. Even schools and colleges and universities, including prestigeous institutions, issue pamphlets and organize courses for the guidance of freshmen students in using contraceptives. The underlying assumption is that fornication between unmarried but consenting adults is, at worst, a tolerable practice. Even certain church leaders speak of the need to change the moral values in view of the modern accepted norms! Detached scientists have demonstrated the damage to our youth that has resulted from this eclipse, in terms of confusion, insecurity and hurt.[20]

I should like to urge all those who share our belief in God to guard themselves against the temptation of imitating these illegitimate premarital practices and to maintain the golden, desirable values of their faiths. I call upon them never to allow themselves to be lured to these immoralities. Seek not to pick your mate through premarital love involving immoral practices. Keep your virginity, maintain your purity and preserve your chastity. The prevalence of a sin does not make it a virtue. You will enjoy your experimentation with your spouse in marriage far more, and will infinitely cherish the feeling of pleasing God both by your premarital chastity and the fulfillment of your marriage. Let not immature passions blind you in making the choice of your mate, to the legitimately recommended qualities which would enhance your happiness

---

[19]According to the recent Redbook Magazine investigation, 90% of married American women admitted having had pre-marital experiences.

[20]See, for example: Thomas J. Cottle, "The Sexual Revolution and the Young", in the New York Times Magazine, November 26, 1972.

in your matrimonial life. A blind love may prove disastrous; and you may realize it only when the flames subside after the wedding, and the discovery of harsh realities about your hasty choice.

Romantic love is an emotional attachment, resulting from sexual attraction, intensified by physical separation. The longing for closeness is intensified by continued separation, lending itself to imaginary exaggeration and affixation of attention upon the beloved—blinded to the shortcomings of the object of love, the realization of which can easily extinguish the lover's passions. The passionate urge seeks fulfillment through closeness by feeding the physical senses on the exaggerated virtues of the beloved, especially by close touching, culminating in copulation.

I do not, however, believe in a romantic Platonic love detached from erotic passions. When the passions are fulfilled repeatedly through easy access of the beloved, the element of exaggeration and imagination is lost and only harsh realities remain, which, as often happens, are below expectations. Now warmth becomes coolness, and passion turns into boredom—even rejection and hatred.[21] Romance should not blind a spouse-seeker to other important qualities which in married life would foster infatuation and increasingly build up durable love and true mutual concern.

Responsible thinkers, alarmed by the disturbing rate of divorce, seriously threatening the stability of the family, trace the roots of this phenomenon to the disparity between marriage expectations and concealed realities among Western couples. While marriage expectation in the East is low, they say, the Western couple's expectation is complex and elaborate. The Eastern husband, they say, looks for sex and sons, and his wife seeks security and sustenance; but the romantic concept of marriage in the West "has pictured it as the panacea for all life's ills and an idyllic state into which

---

[21]Dr. Gerald Albert, a leading professor of psychology and author of "Choosing and Keeping", has concluded after a 40-year period of marriage counselling that "romantic love was being highly overrated, and that the attitude that it is all important has produced disaster for at least one marriage in four and it has caused half of all marriages to be unsatisfactory."

harassed men and women might withdraw from life's struggles to find solace and healing''.[22]

This interpretation is quite questionable. Eastern couples do not seek marriage merely to provide sex and sons for men, and sustenance and security for women. They regard marriage as a significant stage in the development of the individual, an earthly goal of life, attained at maturity. Marriage is like a mission, the fulfillment of which fulfills the individual, and which brings the individual delightful experiences unattainable outside wedlock. These joyful experiences bring the couple closer to each other and steadily heighten their mutual love and infatuation. Before they get bored, they are caught in the occupation of rearing children in whom they see a refreshing replacement of the declining older generation. And thus marriage is a status which is sought not only for personal interests but as a social obligation, which inspires a sense of perpetuity. Within it the individual feels a bond with the past and continuity in the future.

I wonder what a bride and a groom who had courted and fornicated could anticipate from each other more than what each had already learned about the other prior to their marriage ceremony? What differences does the ceremony make? The legal binding, in the circumstances, merely formalizes the already existing relationship, but hardly brings any fresh experiences or new discoveries. Boredom may set in sooner. With easy access to sensual satisfaction outside wedlock through the prevailing permissiveness, and the availability for adoption of illegitimate children, the significance of marriage has diminished. It is in these conditions and in the lack of religious consciousness leading to infidelity, selfishness and impatience with one's spouse that factors of instability of marriages in our time can be located.

To summarize, in the Islamic scheme of marriage, neither man nor woman loses his or her identity. Neither assumes the name of the other. Islam never entertained a doctrine of "femme covert", according to which a woman, on getting married, became no longer a legal person, unable to possess

---

[22]David and Mace, *Marriage East and West* (Doubleday, 1960), p. 294.

property or sign a contract. On the contrary, she always remains an independent, responsible agent like her husband, although both are committed to each other in terms of mutual loyalty and exclusive sexual favors and intimate mutual concern for their common welfare and the welfare of their children. Marriage enhances their maturity, confirms their responsibility, gives them a greater sense of security and provides both with committed, faithful and enduring companionship.

CHAPTER IV
DOMESTIC ROLES AND SEX EQUALITY

Social Status and Personal Roles:

In any given group, be it a clan, a tribe, a club, workers in a factory or in an office or a school, each individual who is a member of the group has a status. From this status a set of duties and obligations emanates. They are incumbent upon the person in that status, and are rights due to his or her fellow-members of the group. The performance and fulfillment of the duties and obligations arising from a status constitute the role which the person who is in that status has to play.

Need For Adjustment:

An individual has as many statuses as the number of the groups to which he belongs. Some of these are inherited, like his position in the family of his birth; and some are acquired, like his status at work. The total of these statuses and the person's ability to adjust and harmonize between the rights and duties arising from them make up his personality and define the quality of his character. The process of adjustment and harmonization may entail also making some sacrifices. For example, personal freedom of action may have to be somewhat curtailed in the interest of the group. This reasonable limitation, such as the prohibition of driving on the left or of parking in certain areas does not conflict with the individual's entitlement to human rights, as it is a slight sacrifice for the sake of the survival of the group with a minimum of conflicts and exposure to danger.

A distinction has to be made, however, between what we may call an "external status" and an "internal status." An internal status is the individual's position and role in the domestic unit, like that of a husband, father, wife, mother or child; and the external status of a person is the total of his positions outside the family unit. Our interest here in the internal status is in that of a husband who may also be a father, and in that of a wife who may also be a mother. A person who remains single, if we disregard his position in the family of his birth, enjoys an external status only; whereas a married person is involved both in an internal and an external status. When the internal and the external statuses overlap as such, a tremendous degree of adjustment involving greater sacrifices must be made for the sake of the smooth living of the domestic unit. Success of this unit, therefore, depends on the ability of each spouse to harmonize and coordinate between the external and the internal roles of each. This, we may emphasize, may entail making enormous sacrifices by either or by both and may impose a minor or drastic modification of their external roles. As much as these sacrifices made in the external role of members of non-domestic groups for the sake of the group's success do not conflict with the concept of universal human rights or the concept of human equality, sacrifices made for the sake of domestic harmony and survival should be regarded in the same way.

Domestic Roles, Possible Alternatives:

Now the question arises as to what pattern of domestic relationship, Islam, as a social legal system, has set up in order to promote the harmony and success of the domestic unit? To put it differently, in what way has Islam sought to harmonize the combined external status and internal role of the husband and those of the wife in a domestic unit in order to ensure its smooth and efficient operation? Before coming to the answer to this question, let us consider some important observations in this context.

The nuptial relationship under which the male status is called "husband", and the female status, "wife", can assume one of four possibilities or arrangements. One possible arrangement is to let the domestic unit live without a team leader, so that the spouses can be equal, neither assuming authority over the other. This, we hardly need to explain, cannot work. The family unit in such circumstances would drift aimlessly like a ship without a navigator, and the children would grow up without a model of authority. Another alternative is to vest the leadership and power over the domestic unit equally in the husband and wife, but this is bound to give rise to chronic disputes and quarrels over the spheres of authority, and the damage to the children under this arrangement need not be emphasized.

Another possible arrangement of the nuptial relationship is to legally vest the power and authority in the wife over the domestic unit, including her husband, but this does not seem to be congruous with the work of nature. To make the gentle woman who is to be loved and adored the source of authority which exudes awe and instills fear and to require her to struggle for her living and for the living of her male partner would be unjust. The dependent male would renege and be relegated from his virile nature to that of a weak, meek creature. Yielding to an aggressive wife, he would have no legitimate outlet for his ego and innate aggressiveness or he might seek unhealthy outlets in drugs and assaults on society. On the other hand, the female, with no dependable power to support her femininity, might suffer a feeling of insecurity and lonesome loss of meaning of the value of life. It is not surprising, therefore, that authority over children in a matrilineal society is vested in the mother's brother, not in the mother. To be a wife is a social status, and to be a husband is another social status. And a social status of a person in a group, as explained above, generates duties which are rights due from that person to the members of that group. In their struggle for survival the members of the social unit have to fulfill basic and other needs, much of which are economic. The leader of the domestic team who assumes authority over its members has to be more perpetually ready to face the domestic problems and protect its members against all dangers. He has to exercise a degree of aggressiveness and toughness, which does not agree with the soft female nature. He has to bear the responsibility of providing shelter and food, which may take him away from home for long or short periods. It does not seem to be fair to impose this domestic leadership and its attending responsibilities upon a creature who is occasionally burdened with pregnancy and the inconveniences of the monthly menstrual discharge.

The Workable Pattern:

The remaining alternative, which is the historical pattern, is to vest the domestic authority in the husband. This is the traditional pattern which has worked efficiently for centuries. Under this arrangement, the husband's role in keeping his wife and protecting his children, a role that can be sustained by physiological and anthropological realities, provides an outlet for man's ego and innate aggressiveness, both physical and sexual. The woman's role of receiving and comforting, on the other hand, agrees and conforms with her gentle nature and provides her with a deep sense of security under the wing of her husband. This pattern of relationship should be regarded as a flexible legal framework within which couples should adjust their special needs according to the circumstances

Under this flexible pattern in which the authority over the domestic unit is vested in the husband, he and his wife share responsibilities within the household, such as the obligation to maintain peace and provide a loving climate. Yet the husband has to be the protective shield and the breadwinner of the family. This pattern of domestic relationship in which the husband plays the role of responsible authority, which should not be abused or exploited against the wife, has been the traditional pattern and the legal form under the law of Islam.

In the past, women hardly had external status. The female's early training was exclusively oriented toward her status as an efficient, loyal and devoted housewife. She did not suffer from the dilemma of and conflicts between an external and internal role. With little difficulty, she could adjust to living with her husband. Until their wedding, she had no experience with other men. On the other hand, a husband could easily adjust to a dedicated wife whose time was devoted to the welfare of the household.

Now, with the opening of the job market to women and expansion of women's education in our times, the traditional balance has been somewhat upset. Many women yearn to pursue a career, and feel that only in pursuing a career can a woman fulfill herself. On the other hand, the absence of the woman from her home while on the job has adversely affected her commitment to her husband and children, and this has badly reflected on domestic stability. Values attached to the traditional pattern have become open to question. It is now argued that a woman has to decide and choose either to pursue a career or be a housewife and mother. With the growing emphasis on sex equality, some even think that this choice has to be made by the male, whether he should be a career man and remain single or a family man giving less time and attention to his job and sparing this to his wife and children.

In my view, the need to choose between pursuing a career and raising a family should not apply to men. There is no inherent conflict between a man's career and his domestic duties. On the contrary, success in his career would enable him to take better care of his dependents. He only has to adjust and find time to share with his wife and children. Here I feel that much depends on the mutual trust and confidence between the spouses and the cultivation of a moral-religious conscience which would play a great deal in promoting this trust.

It is also my view that a woman is entitled to invest her abilities and qualifications in a job that may be open to her. Otherwise, her potentialities which are gifts from God, will lay to waste. However, among the qualities with which a woman is endowed are those which qualify her to be a wife and a mother; and to be a housewife or a mother is by no means less noble than a job outside the home. Therefore, adjustment has to be made between the duties of a woman's job and her domestic obligations with sincere help and cooperation from her husband. A working mother should preferably stay at home to take care of her infant child during his formative crucial years. When he can go to school on his own, a part time job which permits her to see her child off to school and welcome him back on his return would be better than a full time job.

Features of the Recommended Pattern:

Let us now discuss more fully the pattern of conjugal relationship, as recommended in Islam. The following are its main features:

That the couple in the conjugal bond are equal in a permanent partnership;

That the couple, and their children, if any, form a human team;

That the husband is the leader of the team; yet this is not implicit of superiority or inferiority of either spouse;

That the wife is the lieutenant and gentle executive of the team leader;

That love and mutual care and true commitment are the over-riding elements in the relationship;

That each spouse should recognize and appreciate the sensual and psychological needs of the other, and should always endeavor to satisfy those needs, identifying them as his or her own;

That as an aspect of his leadership, the husband is responsible for the protection, the well-being and full maintenance of his wife;

That as a reciprocal duty, the wife has to have regard for the wishes and firm decisions taken by her husband in the interest of the domestic team;

That as a manifestation of his responsibilities and of his love and concern for his wife, the husband is to treat her with esteem, kindness, sympathy, generosity, patience, forgiveness and understanding;

That a wife should not be denied a chance to share in
forming the policy of the household and in making
important decisions affecting the family; and

That the moral growth and the well-being of the children
in general is the mutual responsibility of the parents.

The following texts, some of which were encountered earlier,
are relevant:

"And live with them (women) honorably. If you are
averse to them, it is possible you may be averse to a thing
and God sets in it much good", KORAN IV, 19.

"Live with them honorably, or part with them
honorably." KORAN II, 231.

"No matter how you may try or endeavor, you cannot
do full justice to women. However, be not too unfair to a
wife separating from her with no determined decision.
But if you come to a friendly understanding and practice
self-restraint, God is Forgiving and Merciful."KORAN IV, 129

"Men are in charge of the affairs of their women by
virtue of what God has favored some over the other, and
for what they have expended of their property." KORAN IV, 34

"And (women) have rights equal to the rights incumbent
on them according to what is equitable; and men have a
degree over them." KORAN II, 228.

"Whoever of you whose wife behaves in a disagreeable
manner but he responds by kindness and patience, God
will give him rewards as much as Job will be given for his
forbearance." (Hadith)[1]

"I urge you to treat women kindly. They are a trust in
your hands. Fear God in His trust." (Hadith)[2]

---

[1]Al-Ghazzali, *Op. Cit,* II, P. 39.
[2]Ibn Majah, *Sunan*, vol. 1, P. 594.

"The best of you is he who treats his woman in the best way." (Hadith)[3]

"If I were to require a person to bow to a mortal, I would have urged the wife to bow to her husband." (Hadith)[4]

"Paradise is the reward of a wife who pleases her husband until death." (Hadith)[5]

"The gates of Paradise will be widely open to welcome the woman who observes the mandatory prayers and the fasting of the month of Ramadan and preserves her honor and obeys her husband." (Hadith)[6]

"A woman is nearest to her Lord, (God), when she is inside her home." (Hadith)[7]

"The best of your women is the one who, when her husband looks at her she pleases him; when he beckons to her she obeys him; and when he is away from her she continues to have regard for him, protecting his wealth and perserving her honor." (Hadith)[8]

Reciprocity and Equity:

The husband-wife relationship is thus a reciprocal complementary pattern in which the spouses are equal in dignity and in due respect while their roles and mutual obligations are not necessarily identical. Their roles are best conceived of as attitudes and responsibilities, rather than specific work or activities. Once each party assumes her or his right attitude, it is immaterial what type of work or service each undertakes. The spirit of cooperation and sacrifice by each for the sake of the other should always prevail. It does not matter then which of

---

[3]*Ibid,* P. 636.
[4]*Ibid,* P. 595.
[5]*Ibid.* Cf. Al-Nasa'i, *Sunan,* VI, 11.
[6]Ibn Hibban, *Zawa'id,* Salafiyya Press, 1351 A. H. P. 315.
[7]Ahmad Ibn Hanbal, *op. cit,* VI, P. 297 and 301. Cf. Dailami, *Musnad.*
[8]Ibn Majah, *Sunan,* vol. I, P. 597. Cf. Nasa'i, *Sunan,* VI, P. 68.

them should wash the dishes or make the bed. In case of disagreement, resort may be made to the prevailing customs unless they should entail injustice to either party.

The nuptial role is thus conceived of as a pattern of attitudes and reciprocal responsibilities consistent with the peculiar features of the sex of each spouse. Therefore, part of the role of a wife is to promote an atmosphere of gentleness, grace, warmth, peace, acceptance and obedience, and to undertake of the domestic responsibilities the type of activities which are not too tough for her or would cause her to be away too long from the home. And that of a husband should be an attitude of manliness, giving, generosity, discipline, strength, firmness with understanding and readiness to confront hardship and domestic crises with confidence, wisdom and fortitude.

The conjugal roles are not opposite concepts. They are similar and dissimilar. They have common elements and have different components. They meet and part company. Therefore, husband and wife can share the same type of work. Either or both may cook, wash dishes, vacuum the floor, mend clothes or undertake some repairs. But the wife should be the one who inspires the soft, soothing gentleness; and the husband should be the protective shield, the main source of bread and butter, and the independent, dependable authority. It is this element of authority which is to be respected for the well-being of all in the family and which is spoken of in a Koranic verse quoted above as a degree granted to men over women. It is a degree of responsibility, not a degree of superiority. The husband is made legally responsible for his wife's welfare, her protection and the full cost of her food, her clothes and housing according to her needs and his ability. Muslim jurists state that she is entitled to new clothes for each season. Her food should be provided cooked and ready for consumption. This strictly means that a wife is entitled to fair wages if she cooks and undertakes the task of the household chores. This even applies when she suckles her own child. However, she may choose, as often happens, to forgo such a legitimate claim and regard her labor as her contribution to the needs of the household. In any case, measures should be taken to insure her security in the event of separation.

Within this flexible complementary pattern of conjugal relationship in which the husband leads and is in charge of the wellbeing of his wife and his children, the couple are at liberty to determine any arrangement in having the household work done. They may leave the whole task to a hired service; or either of them may agree to undertake the whole responsibility; or they may agree to share it. After all, the Prophet himself used to share in the household work with his wife. He cleaned, swept the floor, mended clothes and helped in the kitchen. One is inclined, however, to an arrangement in which the wife assumes the responsibility of taking care of the internal affairs of the house, whether a household help is hired or the whole task is shared with her husband in one way or another.

Women and External Work:

In the prevailing conditions of our modern times, women's contributions outside the home are in great demand. This service, depending on the special context of each individual case, does not only provide an additional income to the household, but also relieves the lonely housewife from boredom. With the invention of household gadgets, she enjoys much leisure time with many long hours at her disposal. Delayed marriages nowadays and higher life expectancy for females are additional factors. Moreover, with the universal education of girls and the increasing numbers of qualified women, it would be a lamentable waste to ignore the potentialities of this huge human resource. It would also be an unfair limitation imposed on the liberty of the woman to deprive her of the opportunity to exercise her special abilities, so long as her external services do not upset the home decorum or lead to abusing her dignity. Therefore, we see no objection against a woman engaged in an external job so long as her dignity is respected and she is not unduly exposed. If she is married, her husband's consent is essential.

Permission so granted to women to work outside the home, however, should not be regarded as a denominator of sex equality or a blessed manifestation of modern values. Housewives in the past used to engage themselves in gainful works, the Prophet's wives and daughters included.[9] What is new these days is the modern job discipline and commitment which might interfere with the person's domestic loyalty and therefore involves making rigorous adjustments.

In the past, women could undertake gainful work at home. In modern times, gainful employment brings them forth out of the home. However, while an external job for a woman who can afford it is in our view an honorable and fruitful contribution, yet a housewife who cannot get an outside job owing to her heavy domestic responsibilities should not feel her contribution to be of lower honor or less fulfilling. In fact, nothing is more noble or honorable than being a loving mother and a successful housewife. By staying at home to manage its affairs, the busy housewife keeps it warm, not only physically but more so spiritually and psychologically. She keeps a constant watch over her children, and is better prepared to welcome her husband back from work lovingly and with ready measures of comfort, satisfaction and relaxation.[10]

---

[9]The Prophet used to say: "The most blessed earning is that which a person gains from his own labor."

[10]Mrs. S. Bandaranaike, Prime Minister of Sri Lanka, summarized these thoughts admirably in her statement delivered to the World Women's Conference in Mexico in 1975, in the following words: "What we should strive for is balance and harmony based in the home." She pungently added, "I would be most unhappy if motherhood becomes a dirty word."

CHAPTER V

THE FAMILY AND THE WOMAN'S POSITION

Structure and Function:

The "family" is a social unit, the members of which are united by the strong bond of marriage or blood. The starting point is marriage; and the resulting social unit, a family, consists, in its simple form, of the husband and wife or the husband and wife and their unmarried children. It thus represents one or two generations.

A family consisting of the spouses alone or with their unmarried child or children is known as the simple or "nuclear" family. If the children get married and remain with their parents, bringing in their wives with them in the case of "patrilocal" societies, or their husbands in the case of "matrilocal" societies, the social unit is then known as a "joint" or "extended" family. Consisting of a married couple, their children and their grandchildren, the extended family represents three generations. If the couple or one of them survives and sees the children of their grandchildren, the family then represents four generations.

In the early past, the "extended" family pattern was the only form which would then work. In fact, the family unit was often extended further so as to include all members of the blood group who traced their roots to an ancestor, a real or fictitious ancestor, forming a large human unit anthropologically known as a lineage or clan. They lived in a large compound, consisting of joint families, adjacent to each other and cooperating in their quest for survival.

The large family unit was then self-contained and self-sufficient. Whether it pursued a gathering, agricultural, fishing or mixed economy, the social unit produced the raw material needed for their living and prepared it for consumption. For example, they tilled the land, harvested the product, crushed or ground the corn or wheat, baked the bread, cooked their meals, built their own dwelling and spun and wove their clothes. The large group could afford to do all these activities within itself, sharing the labor and its fruits.

Social progress and civilization reduced the size of the family. It brought about a better but smaller type of dwelling, and provided a finer way of living. The individual became less dependent on his blood group, and there was more room for conflict of interest. Individualism, personal independence and the pursuit of individual ambitions, irrespective of the ancestral interests, were legitimatized. This trend allowed a great deal of maneuverability and enterprise, although women's importance as part of the productive labor force became less. This fact progressively reflected on their status. Yet, the large blood unit did not completely disintegrate. It only gave way from the larger pattern of clan grouping to the relatively smaller type of joint or extended family, in which the individual still identified his interests with those of its other members. The group of "simple" family units which made up an extended family did not need to live under the same roof and mix their food and interests, but they could live adjacently in the neighborhood. The size of houses was a determining factor; and maintaining separate dwellings reduced tension between the in-laws. Yet, the simple nuclear families continued to cooperate in seeking their means of living, and the members took great interest in each other's welfare. Further urbanization and greater mobility tore the simple families apart.

Two points are to be made here: Contiguity between the members of the domestic unit may breed tension, but it is often a mild type tempered by their mutual love and concern, and their tension is easily released and pacified through jokes or apologies. On the other hand, the individual's loyalty to his family need not conflict with his loyalty to the larger groups of which his family is a unit, a clan or village or city. Each has its own scope. Within the family, the individual fulfills his immediate needs. His village or city provides roads and other local services. The state provides health care and security. His obligations to each is commensurate with those services. Thus the family is not to be regarded as a divisive factor. It has always been a training ground and a model in which the individual was equipped to go and struggle efficiently in the wider world.

The institution of the family provides its members with a sense of belonging, inter dependence and of being wanted. The family coordinates the work and activities of its members. Through it, the individual satisfies his biological and psychological needs: namely, food, clothes, shelter, sex, protection and security. The elder generation rears and nurtures the younger ones, and transmits to them their cultural heritage. The parents, willingly and lovingly, take care of their baby, clean its dirt with no resentment, feed it day and night, and protect it from all harm. On the other hand, the family makes a fundamental contribution to society through its reproductive function and the perpetuation of its culture. The family is therefore rightly regarded as the building block of society.

Apart from its tangible, immediate gains, the family also has its extensive and more enduring blessings. Its sensual and individualistic advantages, though legitimate and inestimable, are furtive and short-lived. The reward of its reproductive and cultural services, on the other hand, is more lasting, and the pleasure derived from this is more durable. This is the more appreciated when the individual grows in maturity and age. However, neither aspect should be alone the overriding factor. The family should not be pursued as a factory for the production of babies. Nor should marriage be sought merely for the fun of erotic exercises. Personal fulfillment and reproduction are two objectives which, when combined, invoke the pleasure of God and His more worthy rewards.

When the individual enters into marriage and starts to build a family, he or she should cultivate a balanced set of motives. He should not seek to build a family merely for its individualistic rewards; that is, its economic or erotic values. A human being is not merely a biological unit. He has also a psychological and spiritual entity which seeks to fulfill itself. A sense of responsibility and obligation to others is deeply buried in his soul, although the excitement of youth and its physical vigor may occasionally blind him to this reality. This "altruistic" sense can fulfill itself through service to others, and one of the best measures of doing so is to seek to make a contribution to humanity and its survival through the reproductive, educative and socializing functions of the family.

The Nuclear Family Versus The Extended Family:

Industrialization brought about sweeping and very profound changes in Western society, and its repercussions have been and are being felt in "developing" nations. On the other hand, the recurrent and rapid changes have prepared the mind of the people to accept changes easily and to adapt themselves to them quickly. Resistance to change is now regarded as conservatism and old-fashioned. At the same time, the achievements of industries have changed the quality of human life and have also modified human relations. The need for speedy human mobility has made the simple nuclear family the universally prevailing pattern. The "extended" family pattern is cumbersome and very difficult to move as a unit, and its members could hardly find their modern needs and fulfill their ambitions in one locality. The nuclear family is the type which could fit and was more compatible with the dynamic industrial climate.

Yet, the institution of the family is criticized on the grounds that the nuclear family pattern which fits our industrial ages entails imposition upon the husband, oppression and boredom to the wife, and alienation of the children. The spouses are unnecessarily tied up and limited in their sexual mating. The individual should be left alone, the critics say, to enjoy sex when it would appeal most in its variety of taste. The imposition of a spouse all the time, they claim, leads to boredom and frustration. The city's crowded atmosphere leads to complete isolation and loneliness. The savage competition and the hard work to be put in by the adult male adds to his boredom. The lonely wife cannot find outlets for her suppressed emotions, unlike the olden days when associations with the large membership of the extended family, who were ever present, provided releases for the tensions of the spouses. The children are locked with the mother all the time too closely, and as soon as the father returns at the end of the day, they are put to sleep in their room alone in order to let the father relax undisturbed by their noise. No more grandparents, uncles, aunts or nephews to provide multiple sources for their emotional needs.

I do not see anything inherently wrong with the institution of the family in general or with the nuclear pattern in particular. On the contrary, the latter pattern makes it easier to accommodate a household, as it only needs a reasonable size of housing. More importantly, it inspires the children with an early sense of independence and self-reliance. This early maturity makes them more capable to confront the world's hardships with greater confidence and ability.

The nuclear family can go wrong when it assumes a "detached" attitude. I mean when it concentrates its attention and concern on its internal relationships and becomes self-centered, oblivious to the other members of its kinship. And this seems to be what has happened, and it has brought about serious consequences. It has gradually loosened the ancestral ties, deepened the sense of selfishness, and contributed to the acceptance of the attitude of permissiveness. In turn, these developments brought about grave disasters on the family itself. Let us explain this further.

The internal relationships within the nuclear family unit are: the conjugal relationship between the husband and wife, the parent-child relationship and the siblings relationship, i.e., that existing between brothers, or between sisters or between brothers and sisters. From these three types of relationship is derived a set of mutual rights and obligations, the fulfillment of which helps the domestic ship to sail safely and to achieve its mission. The details of these rights and duties will be discussed later. In the meantime, let us remember that the nuclear family unit is a part of a wider kinship unit, connected by blood or nuptial ties, call it lineage, clan or family. In other words, the concept of the family, depending on the context, may apply to the narrow circle of the nuclear family, as well as to the wider circle which includes all kinsmen and women, related through the paternal or the maternal ancestry.

This bond of kinship no matter how far removed, and no matter how widely its members are territorially dispersed, also entails mutual rights and obligations, involving at least a claim of protection and concerned attention, especially at times of crises. Although the mutual rights and obligations derived from kinship intensify the more we move inwardly from the perimeter of the kinship circle toward the center, those kin removed from that center should also sufficiently capture our attention. In other words, the concept of the extended family, or even the larger one, should be ever present. The individual then cultivates a better and greater sense of belonging, and the internal nuclear family ties become less rigid and less brittle. They will not break easily under tension or pressure. This sense brings greater awareness of a common ancestry and a deeper appreciation of the value of its legitimacy. A member of the group feels to be nourished by a well-balanced nuclear family, buttressed by a supportive network of effective kinship relationships. His emotions are proportionately distributed. Good fortune of one of them brings pleasure to all; and his sorrow is their sorrow. Whenever convenient, they visit each other. They exchange gifts. They correspond. They are ready with protests when one of them feels to be treated by another not according to anticipation, but they settle easily without grudges. Recurrence of such mild frictions adds spice to life, makes it less boring and further consolidates the relationship. The pursuit of strengthening these ties and the fulfillment of their obligations is also an obedience to the religious tenets. If conducted with an awareness of God's presence and His watching and counting of our deeds for greater rewards in an eternal life, the depth of pleasure and satisfaction derived from such achievements is beyond expression.

Compare this non-emotionalized condition to that of a "detached or isolated" nuclear family, as some sociologists describe it. Such a family shrinks within itself. Emotions of its members are concentrated within its limited ties. Yet, the few on whom a member depends may be too busy to provide the needed attention. The ambition of the father is to achieve material sucess. The mother, with no company most of the day, is bored by the routine climate at home and resentful of the rigid role which stifles her potentiality. The spiritual values which harmonize and ennoble the conjugal relationship are absent. The goal is only materialistic and the pursuit of the pleasure here and now. There is less or no interest in ancestry or in its legitimacy. Artificial insemination is easily resorted to. Extra-marital activities for diversion are tolerated. Children experience no more the control which was exercised by the presence of members of the extended family, and religion is no longer a restraining force. Loose conduct for unbounded sensual satisfaction is tolerated by a neighborhood uninterested in what others may do. Children have no concept of deep ancestral roots. They are confronted with double-standard situations in their parents' behavior. So they mistrust them and disrespect them. They strive but fail to find a meaning for life, and then they may seek to induce illusions of a meaning through drugs and unhealthy activities.

Yet the nuclear family pattern is indispensable in modern industrial societies; but its members have to diversify their ties, particularly with their kin. They should keep close interest in them and seek to fulfill their obligations to them. Moreover, they should cultivate and improve their religious sense through determined repentance and constant awareness of God and through sincere and devoted prayers, not only in a temple on the day of Sabbath, but always, all days and anywhere they happen to be. God loves his creatures, it is true. Yet God is not only a lover and a redeemer. He wants us to lead a really happy and secure life with a minimum of hatred, disputes, stresses and confusion. And this can be attained by obedience to His law and by not over-estimating this life as to forget the value of the life to come. Success in that greater life depends on the degree of obedience to the divine law. And one of God's teachings is to observe the rights of one's kin. The Koran repeatedly emphasizes noble treatment of kin, making it next to God's own right and the parent's right. And the Prophet once said that a neglected kin complained to God against his inattentive relative although he was remote from him by forty degrees.

Future of the Traditional Family Pattern:

The recommended nuclear family pattern, as described, with diversified ties in a wider circle of kin, sanctioned and sanctified by Holy ordinances and sincere obedience to these divine teachings, is the practical alternative to the existing confusion. I strongly believe that the traditional family pattern based upon marriage and blood relationship shall survive and triumph.

Reference has been made to the severe attacks on the institution of the family as well as on marriage these days and the call for alternatives in which people break loose from all traditions. The relative success of the "social" father or mother, as substitutes for the natural parents in the absence of either has encouraged some writers to propose a type of "family" not based on blood or marriage relationship, such as baby farms in which babies could be taken care of by trained sympathetic nurses. Some suggest that such baby farms or nurseries should be of small size so that the babies can receive greater individual attention, and they themselves could develop closer "sibling" relationships. Women, and men, should enjoy sex for its own pleasure when they want and with whom each may want. And when a woman gets herself impregnated deliberately or casually and delivers a baby she would deposit it in the baby farm or nursery. This arrangement, in the opinion of its proponents, would take care of the need of sexual satisfaction and the need of human reproduction.

Enough has been said already in this volume about the value of marriage as a permanent, dependable commitment. As for "social" parenthood to substitute for the natural parent, it cannot be accepted as a universal alternative. The "social" parent substitute could only achieve a partial success in the relatively rare cases of the absence of the natural parent who is responsible for the birth of the child. The relative success of the "social" substitute is due to its rarity and to the fact that it operates in a climate in which the natural traditional parenthood dominates. The "social" substitute, resorted to in the case of the absence of the natural agent seeks to emulate the traditional norms and to cultivate emotions similar to those of the original parent. I am not opposed, however, to the creation of nurseries that would take partial care of legitimate children when needed, so long as the real parents dominate in nurturing their child and so long as the child enjoys enough hugs from the warm breast of his mother and the loving arms of his father.

The increasing number of non-family households in recent years occupied by single persons or by unmarried couples or communes does not agitate against the institution of the family. This phenomenon only reflects the current permissive attitude, the loss of spiritual motivation and the weakness of the kinship ties. I strongly feel that this permissive attitude and the related practices constitute a transitory phase which will eventually lead, after universal awareness of its futility and damaging effect, to a swing back to the traditional values and to a healthy family pattern. People are already tired of the outrageous practices and are yearning for the revival of the precious traditional setup.

The major factors leading to family instability and the rising rate of divorce can be summarized in the following elements. Our current individualistic spirit which rates personal interests and pleasure over other considerations leads to conflicts and injurious misunderstandings, as personal interests and motivation do not often agree. Permissiveness and easy mixing between the sexes alienates one spouse from the other and provokes jealousies and deep bitterness. The national affluence and the availability of gainful jobs has broken the feeling of inter-dependence between the members of the household, which in the past played an effective role in sustaining domestic solidarity. Disregard of the enduring considerations in making one's choice of a mate, and the total independence of the young marrying couple, not benefiting from the wisdom and experience of their parents in making the selection, are additional factors. A couple brought together merely by a blind love are likely to discover soon after marriage their incompatibility, and their struggle to maintain the nuptial tie may not be successful. The social and spiritual isolation of the family, the religious vacuum, and the pressures and strains of the modern crowded life, make the egocentric pleasure-seeking spouse very brittle and edgy, incapable of sustaining himself against the blows of domestic strains.

Lack of deep religious conviction and turning away from spiritual values that would sustain and reinforce the blood ties uniting remote kin has contributed to marriage instability. Cohesion between these kin always needed external pressures in order that they be welded together. When the extended family model gave way to the nuclear pattern, tearing apart the ties with remote kin, the emotional life of the members turned inward and centered on the few members of the simple family unit. Rejection as well as too much affection are harmful. Loyalty to the machine and faith in science and technology have weakened the religious life and given way to irresponsible liberty which has led to objectionable new "life styles", such as "group marriages," and alarming increases in the number of illegitimate births. It was not accidental therefore that the rebellion of the youth and women's liberation movement—both of which seek opening to the world—came simultaneously with the advent of the so-called "sexual revolution".

These destabilizing factors are not inherent in human nature, nor are they insurmountable. I believe that they are merely symptoms of the phase of change which we have been enduring through the last few decades. It seems also to be a phase reaction to a rigid concept of the sanctity of marriage as an insoluble bond unto death. Calm and sobriety are bound to prevail; and when people are restored to their moral and religious heritage the institution of the family will regain its strength.

Internal Family Organization:

It was explained earlier that there are three major operative relationships within the family: the conjugal relationship, the parent-child relationship and the siblings relationship.

The success of the family in achieving its objectives, namely: satisfaction and security of its members and its reproductive, cultural contribution to society, depends on the degree of harmony and coordination of the interaction of these three relationships and the harmonious way in which mutual rights and obligations arising therefrom can work.

The best way to ensure the harmony and flexibility which lead to stability and successful coordination is to look at these relations and the obligations derived from each of them as patterns of attitude which, in matters of details, should respond to needs and situations. As such, the total pattern becomes a resilient network that can assume a working shape in changing situations.

Reference has been made to the patterns of conjugal relations based on the principle of sex equality and the reality of sex differences. Based on the former principle, the couple should treat each other with equal regard, love, concern and constant attention. A "job" occupation or work engagement should not lead to inattentiveness or indifference by one toward the other. Spouses are equally responsible for rearing the children and bringing them up in a good responsible way. However, the status of the male spouse is that of husband-father and the status of the female spouse is that of wife-mother. Therefore, these equally important roles cannot be identical or the same but reciprocal and complementary. This is derived from the reality of sex differences. The wife-mother's role in exuding charm, a delightful loving air, close and warm gentle care, on the other hand, complements the husband's role as the loving attentive firm shield, the main wellspring of provision of the domestic needs and protection from the external world, and the ever-present image of discipline, hard work and self-control.

The principle of mutual consultation between spouses can be illustrated from historical noble examples. Records show that the Prophet himself consulted his spouse over important problems, and was to a great extent dependent upon this affection and intellectual support of his wife. We may recall the fears and doubts which gripped his mind when he received his first revelation, and how he was then reassured and sustained by his wife, Khadijah. In the many long and lonely years of severe persecution meted out against him, it was the same gracious wife who did not only lend him protection but also provided him with a soothing support until she died. In later years, the wise counsel and companionship of his next wives were a tremendous source of strength to the Prophet in tackling his great responsibilities.

As part of the scheme of the internal domestic relations as prescribed by God, which is clearly designed to ensure harmony and promote mutual love and devotion so that the basic social unit—the family—the pillar on which the nation and its survival rests, should function properly and efficiently, the general Islamic guidelines of human relations applies; namely, that the older and the stronger should have mercy on the younger and the weaker, and the younger should respect and obey the older.

> "He is not one of us who does not have mercy on the younger, or does not respect the older", said the Prophet.[1]

The parent-child relationship is of a dynamic nature. First, it consists of a complete helpless filial dependence and fully intense emotional parental selfless concern and protection. It has no element of reciprocity in the early part of the life of the child. Interaction gradually grows when the child grows and begins to manifest the result of the early stage of acculturation and socialization in terms of awareness and partial independence. Here he begins to bear a degree of responsibility which should take the form of obedience and compliance. Parents here should be aware of the vital importance of this critical formative stage. The child needs to be trained in self-reliance and creativity, and to be imbued with the impression of being surrounded by a friendly but occasionally resisting world. It is now believed that the child's age from the eighth month to the eighteenth or the twentieth is of crucial importance in his rearing. The parent-child relationship pattern shifts when the child becomes of age, at which point he or she becomes a fully responsible agent. Until then, parents, especially the father, were responsible for his shelter, clothes and other expenses. Such parental obligations, however, extend to dependent daughters until they are married and to dependent sons who are in school.

---

[1]Abu Dawud, *Sunan,* vol. IV, p. 421.

Reciprocity as an element in the parent-child relationship grows in degree and intensity according to the life cycles of the parent and the child. As soon as he begins to understand and discriminate, the child has to maintain an obedient and respectful attitude toward his parents. The more he grows in strength, physically and financially, the more the parent declines in health and self-sufficiency, the more the child should become helpful and understanding toward his parents. The wisdom of the parents should be sought at the time of a crisis, and at no time should they be neglected or treated with indifference. More details will come when we speak about "filial duties".

The pattern of siblings' relationship is one of equality, love, and mutual regard and concern. This pattern also should allow some flexibility in order to meet the need of shifting situations with the growth in age and strength by the younger siblings and the decline of the older ones.

This resilient network of domestic relationship which always assures cooperation in accordance with the needs, and in which both the family interests and the interests of the individual members are harmonized, could withstand social changes easily and survive shifts and upheavals.

Factors Cementing Family Ties:

The close ties within the inner circle of kinship are further reinforced in Islam by legal ordinances pertaining to inheritance, exogamy and the rules of personal privacy. This is not the place to discuss these legal aspects in detail, but our purpose is to draw attention to them as measures inculcating a greater sense of close relationship and mutual concern.

A woman, under the Islamic law, cannot marry her father, her son, her father-in-law, her son-in-law, her brother, her paternal or maternal uncle, or the son of a brother or sister.

It is also not allowed for a couple of different sex to be alone in private or to see of each other except the parts which can be exposed in public; but this rule is relaxed in the case of a couple unmarriageable to each other under the law. Prohibition then applies only to the parts between the knees and the navel. This relative concession assumes that the sexual passion does not normally arise between two exogamous parties, no matter what Freud and others may say. A couple that allows themselves incestuous behavior can be nothing but perverted animals.

The Islamic law of inheritance is complex; but the following are some of its relevant features:

> i) The surviving spouse of the deceased, the surviving parent or parents, and all the surviving sons and daughters must share in his or her estate.

> ii) All surviving sons of the deceased get equal shares; the elder gets as much as the younger one. The same can be said in the case of daughters.

> iii) All surviving brothers, full, paternal or maternal, and their sisters share in the estate under certain conditions. The same applies to paternal uncles and their sons.

Details of the distribution of the estate and shares of the heirs are beyond the scope of this work.

We have discussed these legal ordinances which are mutually applicable between members of the inner circle of the kinship group, just in order to demonstrate their value in further consolidating the bonds uniting these members. These mutual legal obligations, in addition to the rich spectrum of moral guidance pertaining to domestic life, make the members of the domestic unit feel they are in a special category, whose members are interdependent and closely knit together, and each of them stands in a special significant status to the others.

If you can build each family on such strong foundations of wholesome sentiments, you are indeed a builder of a society of peace and optimum happiness, a society in which life is more meaningful and the individual enjoys a true sense of "belonging" and significance.

Value of Child Bearing and Rearing:

The importance of properly nurturing the children cannot be overemphasized. The human offspring is reproduced, not as goods manufactured in a factory or a laboratory, or like an animal born in a barn, but as a dignified being whose appearance is welcome and whose troubles are handled with patient willing care and affectionate concern. Some people marry in response to inner or social pressures. As for a responsible citizen, the overriding consideration in getting married and seeking to beget children is to satisfy his conscience and to fulfill God's will. Reproduction, coupled by the intention to protect one's chastity in obedience to God, is his primary motivation. He craves for children not for having fun, or in order to perpetuate his name, or to substitute the declining generation of his parents or to re-live his own childhood, but to make a meaningful contribution to society and to please God by obeying His command and to be worthy of His rewards by accepting the burden of taking good care of his own family. The Prophet, addressing the youth, said:

"Get married, reproduce and let your number increase."[2]

And the Koran reads:

"And God has made for you mates of your own nature;
and made for you, out of them, children and grandchildren; and provided for you sustenance of the best."
KORAN XVI, 72.

In our time, some couples undesirous of having children take drastic measures to avoid the occurence of conception altogether. Selfish interests or the fear of added responsibilities may be the motive for this attitude. In some cases, a career woman may be so devoted to her job that she prefers not to interrupt it by pregnancy, delivery and child care. Some wives, misguided by a biased interpretation of the concept of liberation advocated by some extremist activists, hesitate to reproduce until such a time when the husband would mother

---

[2]Ibn Majah, *Sunan*, I, 592 & 595.

the child or at least bear an equal share of mothering him.

It is unbecoming of a reasonable, sensible person to run away from the responsibility of rearing children in order to be completely free for selfish pursuits. And to fear the burden of bringing up a child is inconsistent with the virtuous attitude of cultivating confidence in God and relying upon Him. The Koran reads:

> "If they (the couple) are in poverty, God will give them means out of His grace; for God is all-encompassingly Generous and is All-Knowing!" KORAN XXIV, 32

And the Prophet says:

> "If you really rely upon God, He will provide for you as He provides for the birds. They fly out of their nests with empty stomachs, seeking their provision, and return with full stomachs."[3]

A woman's job outside the home is by no means more fulfilling than becoming a successful mother. What can a job bring to the person when that person perishes after years of uninterrupted hard toil? Success in a job cannot be impaired by interruptions of two, five, or even ten years in order for a woman to fulfill herself as a mother. There are brilliant women in their 60's whose grown-up children have established successful homes but still hold to their own senior job positions.

Rearing the children is a noble responsibility which is to be shared by both parents, but the cost of which is part of the father's share. If the mother carries out the burden she is entitled for reward under the Islamic law. This includes breastfeeding of the child. The Koran reads in this respect:

> "And the Mothers shall give suck to their children for two full years if they desire to complete the term, but the fathers shall bear the cost of their provision and clothing on equitable terms. No soul shall have a burden laid on it greater than it can bear; nor shall a mother be treated unfairly on account of her child." KORAN II, 233.

---

[3]Ibn Majah, *Sunan,* II, 1394.

It also reads:

> ". . . and if they suckle your children, give them their recompense." KORAN LXV, 6.

Although there is no hard and fast line of division as to the distribution of the housework and the spouses may choose any arrangement that they may like to follow, the child in its early life is more attached to his mother. I believe in the validity of a motherly instinct which impels her to cuddle him, to hold the child close to her bosom, to find pleasure in cleaning him, and to respond with immense pleasure when he looks healthy or with deep concern when he suffers sickness.

Factors of Domestic Instability:

There has been a deep concern over the deteriorating conditions of the family, manifested in a rapidly increasing high rate of divorce and a grave generation gap. From the above analysis, however, it can be gathered that the current disequilibrium stems from abusing the principle of personal freedom and the absence of a deep religious commitment. The situation is further aggravated by the daily separation of the members of the family during the school and working hours and the prolonged gap between the physical maturity of the children and their attainment of economic independence.

Domestic stability is dependent upon the smooth working of the internal relationships within the family and the fulfillment of the obligations derived from these relationships. This entails a degree of restraint and making some sacrifices, which is inconsistent with loose conduct and unrestricted liberty. Moreover, the daily separation of the members of the family does not only lead to alienation but also provides chances for destructive peer influences. Furthermore, children nowadays attain physical maturity earlier than before, but their economic independence is much delayed by years of education and special training in order to fulfill the high ambitions of their parents. During this prolonged 'adolescence', the children remain dependent upon their parents and supposedly subject to their control which runs against the natural demands of their physical maturity. This naturally leads to deep resentment by the children, and even rejection, revolt and horrifying disrespect of their parents.

By contrast, children in the past attained economic independence earlier. They effectively participated in the work of their family farm or family shop, and their financial contribution was recognized almost about the time when they became physically mature. Thus they were able to meet their sensual needs in time. Parents did not feel disillusioned in their children nor did the children suffer from a sense of insecurity that could arise from failure to fulfill their parents' anticipations.

The demands of the modern age are inevitable. Yet, domestic harmony and stability can still be achieved if the members of the family exercise self restraint and respect their moral duties stemming from their domestic bonds and their commitment to God and His divine law. Admittedly this is much harder than it used to be, but the rewards are very much worth the struggle.

Adoption of Children:

With the increasing number of children born out of wedlock, the need for adopting "parents" is getting greater and greater. On the other hand, childless couples may be motivated in adopting a child by their desire to fulfill their "parental instinct", if there is such an instinct. Some others adopt children with the intention to use them when they grow in such pursuits as domestic service. Still some others are motivated in adopting children by a charitable urge. They wish to deliver an orphan, for example, from the ravishes of deprivation and to bestow upon him "parental" love and care.

Is adoption a permissible practice under the Islamic law? The answer depends on the definition of adoption. If it entails full integration of the adopted child into the family so that the baby becomes for all purposes a son or daughter of the adopting couple, called after their name and entitled to all the rights of a real child, the practice is certainly prohibited. The Prophet was given as a gift a slave boy called Zayd by his first wife. He emancipated him, adopted him and called him Zayd, son of Muhammad. This was before Muhammad, peace be upon him, received his Prophetic call. Later, the following Koranic words were revealed:

"God has not made as your own children those you call after your name. Such is only the speech of your tongues. But God tells you the truth and He guides to the right path. Call them after the names of their real parents. This is more just in the sight of God. If you do not know the real parents, they are simply your brethren and clients." KORAN XXXIII, 4-5

On the other hand, if adoption simply means taking the baby who does not belong to you into your custody in order to bring him or her up without identifying him or her as yours, no welfare state or sensible system may object to it. Such a child will not and should not automatically have the same rights as those of a real child under the Islamic law. You may grant him any portion of your property during your lifetime. Or you may bequeath to him or her up to one-third of your estate. But he will not have a right of inheritance. Islam is concerned in keeping descent unmixed and unconfused.

Whatever the moral or the legal value of the Islamic prohibition of full adoption may be, the acceptable partial adoption in which the child is not given the name of the adopting couple or granted the legal rights due to the real child is far better, safer and more meaningful. Recent research has revealed the traumatic results of sealing the records of the adopted child. The air of secrecy about their origin is repressive both for the adoptive and the real parents. Besides, there are other evils involved. Apart from hiding a truth, jealousies, hatred and disputes are likely to arise between the adopted person and the real children of the adopting parent or parents. The idea behind the secrecy; namely, to break the relationship between the adopted child and his real parents and make him an integral part of his adoptive family is of no real advantage. In the words of a family law specialist, it is "merely an attempt to elevate a legal fiction to a natural fact, and it just isn't working."[4] This secrecy is likely to lead to grave errors. A young couple were to be wed to each other recently in New York, unknowing that the prospective bridegroom was the natural brother of the prospective bride, who had been adopted at birth.[5]

Parental Obligations:

A child should be given a good name at birth; and should be taken good care of until it grows and matures. Although the natural parental instinct conduces the parents to treat their children kindly, Islam has established legal safeguards against the possibility of a degenerate parent abusing his child. As a sign of regard, the child is to be greeted on the 7th day after his birth with a welcoming feast for which a lamb or a larger animal should be sacrificed. The words of the call to prayers should be recited in both ears after its safe delivery; and if it is a boy, he should be circumcised preferably on the day of the feast party, the seventh day after his birth.

Parents should help their children to build up an independent dynamic character. They should also help them build up their inner strength based upon the dynamics of a righteous relationship with God. In a land where Islam is a small minority, the need for good models of Muslim parents is much greater. Muslim practices and Muslim habits, even those which may not appear to be significant, are very much so in that context. In the American setting, children should be trained for living in a pluralistic society, of racial variety and religious diversity. Our faith has set a model of tolerance and understanding in the history of mankind. It does not condemn innocent adherents of other religions, and it respects and believes in all the past Prophets and in their missions. And it is God's will to create people different. Our Holy Book reads:

> "If your Lord had so willed, He would have made all mankind one nation . . ." KORAN XI, 117

---

[4] Winston Groom, "Adopted Children", *The Washington Star,* December 7, 1975.

[5] *Ibid.*

Unless children possess wealth from such sources as inheritance or work, the cost of their living is obligatory on their father. This obligation, according to the law of Islam, applies until the male child becomes of age, and the daughter is married. If the child is a full-time student, the obligation on the able father continues even after the son becomes of age. It also continues after the son's attainment of the age of legal adulthood if he is physically incapable to work and earn his living.

If the father is financially unable to bear the cost of living for his child, the obligation is transferred to the grandfather. If there is no grandfather or he is unable to meet the obligation, it is transferred to the able brother or uncle, if there is either. In case there is none, the cost of living for the child has to be met by the Muslim treasury.

The father, apart from this material obligation, has, in collaboration with the mother, to rear the child in a healthy way, physically and culturally. Children, our own as well as others, have to be treated with affection, gentleness and understanding. The Prophet, peace be upon him, used to play fondly with the children, not only at home but even in the streets and in the mosque. He sat them on his lap and let them fumble with his fingers. He allowed them to ride on his back while he was kneeling in prayers.[6]

A light punishment may be applied to a child in case of disobedience, but it should never be too harsh. Parents should be neither permissive nor too authoritarian, but reasonably disciplinary, in order to give the children a sense of limits and boundaries and a feeling of protection and security. Overly indulgent parents give the child an impression of indifference and make him unsure of himself. On the other hand, authoritarian parents may strangle the child's personality. A moderate course is always wiser.

In bringing up a child, parents should help him develop a core of self-control and self-respect, and the attitude of striking a midway, balanced course in dealing with problems— neither violence nor self-defeating docility. Response to an

---

[6]Ibn Hanbal, *Musnad,* vol. IV, No. 99.

insult, for example, should neither be hysterical nor stooping, but a calm reaction that seeks to correct the aggression. Islam is a religion which chooses the middle path. It is opposed to taking an extreme position. The Koran reads:

> "And thus have We made you a nation justly balanced."
> KORAN II, 143.

Islam does not teach turning the left cheek when one is struck on the right cheek; nor does it teach that the victim should strike back. It teaches that justice has to be redressed in the proper lawful way. In this respect, the Koran reads:

> "The response to an aggression is like punishment; yet
> whosoever forgives and makes peace, his reward is one
> from God. Verily God loves not the aggressors. And
> he who retaliates for a wrong that has been done to him,
> verily he is not to be blamed." KORAN XLII, 40-41

Children are very impressionable, and nothing builds up their characters, for better or for worse, than the model set up for them by their own parents. It is therefore true to say that the child is the mirror which reflects his parents. The parents therefore should set a good model of behavior in front of the child. They should not quarrel in front of them, or get ill-tempered too quickly over trivial matters, or allow fits of anger to reveal their pitfalls to the children.

If you have more than one child, the siblings have to be treated equitably. Favoring one over the other provokes destructive jealousies. Once a man went to the Prophet, peace be upon him, and requested him to bear witness that he had given his child a gift of an orchard. The Prophet asked him, "Do you have another child?" The man said, "Yes." The Prophet asked: "Have you given him an equal gift?" "No," he said. The Prophet answered: "I do not bear witness to an injustice."[7]

The necessity of avoiding any acts that may appear to be discriminatory by parents applies even at the infant stage of

---

[7]Muslim, *Sahih*, II, 7/8. Cf. Ibn Majah, *Sunan*, II, 795.

the child. I am not a believer in the Freudian conjectures, but jealousy is easily provocable, and it may leave deep scars on the mind of the child who is hurt early. Parents with one child, who absorbs their attention, should be careful when the mother conceives another. The existing child should be made to anticipate with pleasure the "intruder" who is to share their attention. The same applies to more than one child in the case of future conception. Tell the existing child that a baby is being made to play with him or with her, and this impression should become more intensified with the approach of delivery. Let him or her share with you in a playful way the preparations and even the purchase of articles for the coming baby. Give him whatever toys you may get for the baby and let him hand them over to the baby. Also let him share in cleaning it and clothing it; and let him or her take care of it alone, with you watching from afar. This may hopefully reduce the provocation of jealousy.

An important point to be borne in mind by parents is that the process of change is always at work, and therefore they should take into account that their child will be mainly living in a different generation. The great Imam Ali, the cousin and son-in-law of the Prophet, used to say:

"Do not compel your children to accept your manners.
They belong to a generation different from yours."[8]

This advice was uttered more than thirteen centuries ago, when changes were not so rapid. It is the more needed in our age. Another popular word of wisdom says:

"When your son matures, treat him as a brother."

Therefore parents should respect the independence of their adult children. They should offer them advice, but should not seek to impose their views upon them, particulary in matters of their own personal interest.

---

[8]*Nahj al-Balaghah,* (with commentary of Ibn Abi 'l-Hadid,) Halabi Press, Cairo, 1967, 2nd. ed., vol. XX, p. 267.

Filial Duties:

As much as parents have to take good care of their children, the children should treat their parents with honor, love and respect. The Koran reads:

> "And your Lord has decreed that you should worship
> none but Him, and that you should be kind to your
> parents. If one or both of them should attain old age in
> your life, never say a word of contempt or anger to them
> and never do anything that may hurt them but address
> them in terms of honor. And lower unto them, out of
> mercy, the wing of humility, and say: 'My Lord! Bestow
> on them Your Mercy, as they had nurtured me in
> childhood." KORAN XVII, 23/4

Other Koranic verses and statements made by the Prophet have been quoted, in which noble treatment of parents, especially the mother, is urged. Apart from this dutiful moral treatment of the parents, children have to bear the living cost of their needy parents, whether they live together or apart. If a child can afford to sustain only one of his living parents, the mother is to be given preference. However, parents' sustenance should be borne without a trace of resentment or grudge and must be accompanied by willing signs of respect and warm regard and affection. In case of the absence of an able child, maintenance of a grandparent is obligatory on his or her grandchildren.

An important point which must be borne in mind is that the obligation of bearing the living costs of a child by a parent and vice-versa, applies whether the payee and receiver are of the same religion or of different faiths. In other words, it makes no difference whether either party is a Muslim and the other is a non-Muslim.

It is my opinion that when parents grow old, they should live with their children or close to them. To put them in a nursing home or in a senior citizen's institution is an unbearable isolation. It makes them feel rejected, useless, insignificant and unwanted. It looks to them as if they remain there only to wait for death. Moreover, surrounded by people of similar gloomy fate, they suffer painful boredom and the agonies of isolation. On the other hand, when they live close to their children the bond uniting them with the world of hope is unsevered, and their energy can also be revamped by sharing in the pleasures and sorrows of the younger members of their family. Never mind if sometimes they may quarrel, and then make up for their misunderstanding. This way, time goes by more quickly, and life becomes more meaningful and enjoyable. Their presence connects the past with the future, while their wisdom and experience may be sought for guidance and help in time of crisis. When they get sick they find themselves surrounded by people who have warm affection and true concern for them; and when they pass away they go in dignity, remembered with eager prayers and sincere thoughts. The Prophet, peace be upon him, said:

"When a person dies, nothing more can benefit him except three things: A perpetual charity he started; some useful knowledge he had contributed; and the prayers of a righteous child."[9]

Next to the conjugal family tie and the parent-child relationship comes the siblings' bond. Brothers and sisters are bound together in a strong mutual responsibility. We may recall here the Prophet's words in which he acclaimed the merits of a brother who takes good care of his needy sisters. Also, mutual obligations of protection, moral and financial help between brothers are overwhelming, and the same is true between sisters. Similar obligations are extended between children of the siblings. This pattern of closeness is also manifested in certain legal considerations.

Further Emphasis on the Mother's Right:

Consistent with the difference in the role played by each party of the conjugal couple in bringing forth the child, the wife is granted a greater right as a parent than that due to her husband. From the moment of conception until delivery, she

---

[9]Muslim, *Sahih,* II, 14.

carries the baby always, till delivery. She may breastfeed it for two years or so. She is never loath to cleaning the child and washing its dirt. Therefore, her right over the child as a mother is much more emphasized in Islam than that of the father, as we may have gained from texts quoted earlier. In this context let us also reflect upon the following Koranic passages:

> "And We have enjoined upon man to do good to his parents. His mother bears him with trouble and she brings him forth in pain. And the bearing of him and the weaning of him is thirty months." KORAN XLVI, 15.

> "And We have enjoined on man concerning his parents—his mother bears him with weakness over weakness, and his weaning takes two years, saying: 'Give thanks to Me and to your parents. To Me is the eventual return.' "KORAN XXXI, 14.

And as a mother, the woman's share in the estate of her deceased child is categorically assured. Without going into the complexities of the law of inheritance in Islam, let us read these Koranic words:

> ". . . and to each of his parents one-sixth (of the estate is due) if there is a (surviving) child (of the deceased person.) If there is no child of the deceased person and his parents inherit his wealth, his mother's share is one third." KORAN IV, 11

Again, in recognition of the greater role of the mother in bringing forth the child, her right in the custody of her children is duly acknowledged. Unless she is morally disqualified or is remarried, she is automatically granted custody over her children if she is separated from their father, until at least the male child's age is seven and that of the female becomes nine. Then the child chooses whether to remain with the mother or to move in with the father. Throughout the period of the custody under her, the mother is entitled to fair wages for taking care of the child. The father

edges. Elevated and sublimated, it helps build happy domestic relations. Abused and misused, it is degrading and humiliating, especially to women. All extra-marital, pre-marital and 'ultra-marital' diversions and perversions are damaging, destructive and, in my own opinion, are incongruous with human dignity. Equally or more importantly, all these deviations are sins against the teachings of God and they invoke His displeasure.

Researches seeking biological, genetic, hormonic, hereditary, anthropological or environmental factors of sexual perversions may have their academic value. However, their result will not alter the moral or religious judgment of these practices. From earliest times, it has always been recognized that the individual is born with opposing sets of motives. One set pulls him to evil and the other promotes good deeds and endeavors to keep away from evils. Hence, he is privileged with the provision of brains, intelligence, sharp perception and a discriminating conscience. The merit of the individual, as a human being, depends on the degree of his ability to resist the evil forces and listen to the dictates of his conscience and those of his Lord. If we were to follow inborn inclinations wherever they may lead us, with no blame or stigma, what would then be the value of the virtue of self-control which is counted as one of the most noble human characteristics? What difference would there be between a person given to sensual pleasure, unrestrained by his conscience or by a religious adherence, and an animal which is only moved by its instincts? It is on account of the fact that man has to struggle against seductive forces to attain purity that man is regarded to be a degree higher than the angels who are believed to be created without evil motivations and are therefore sinless.

Human beings are susceptible to failure, however, and God is there to forgive or to bring the sinner to account. Yet the Koran emphasizes the divine qualities of God as being Compassionate, Merciful and Forgiving.[17]

---

[17]It is worthy to note here that the Koranic Term describing God as Forgiving occurs 190 times. That denoting His Mercy and Compassion is repeated almost 400 times; whereas derivatives of the root meaning that He is Revengeful (of sinners) occurs only thirteen times.

Therefore, a private violation of the moral conduct is not of much concern to us. Responsible conscientious people are very disturbed by the wide publicity of un-Biblical and un-Koranic sexual attitudes in all their varieties and the attempt to elevate them to the level of normality and permissibility, thus outrageously violating the moral conscience and the teachings of God, and contributing to the breakdown of the family.

This is not self-righteousness or a case of double-standard attitude. One wonders why this accusation is leveled only against a person who may fail under seductive temptations but keeps his sin a private matter between himself and his Lord to Whom he may repent and from Whom he may seek forgiveness. Why are such terms so popular in describing the call for abstention from publicity on sexual misconduct and are not so used in wide-spread corruption, deception and other criminal acts and outrageous violations? The wide publicity of corrupt sex practices, the public shows of X-rated films and the unrestrained lewd pornography, all of which are manifestations of the so-called "Sex Revolution", are certainly harmful and destructive social diseases. Sober scientists have demonstrated the damage to our youth that has resulted from this "revolution" in terms of confusion, insecurity and hurt.[18]

Sex Education:

The discussion of sex leads us to the subject of sex education. In view of the current attitude of permissiveness, and the easy mixing of boys and girls in schools, in offices, in factories and elsewhere, youngsters have become exposed to certain dangers,[19] and some responsible thinkers have felt the need to educate them in the area of sex so that they could take

---

[18]Thomas J. Gottle, "The Sexual Revolution and the Young", *The New York Times Magazine*, November 26, 1972.

[19]It is said that six out of each ten teenage mothers are unmarried or get married after they become pregnant. Over 70% of them did not use contraceptives and 55% thought they were too young to become pregnant.

good care of themselves. One may question, however, the real value of sex education as a separate subject.

To institute a special discipline of sex education, in my view, is unnecessary and to include in such courses the teaching of sex techniques is unethical and unbecoming to human dignity. The scientific value of sex education is taken care of in such disciplines as biology and physiology which are parts of the regular school curricula. To create a separate discipline for that in the regular school or in weekend classes would unduly lend greater emphasis on the sensual value of the subject and create an unhealthy climate of sexual provocation among the adolescents. Moreover, courses designed for sex education tend to ignore the ethical aspect of sex and pay special attention to teaching birth control methods to adolescent people, thus giving the unmarried youngsters the wrong impression that pre-marital activities are acceptable so long as pregnancy is avoided and protective measures against sexually transmitted diseases are taken.

I am particularly opposed to the teaching of so-called "sex techniques" to unmarried adolescents. When they get married, the intelligent couple by themselves or with the help of available literature can learn and create methods and techniques and settle on the methods and positions that suit them best. The teaching of such details, in open discourse, offends the element of privacy inherent in the act, and thus causes it to lose its mystical touch and deprives it of its magically limitless taste. And when this teaching is accompanied by illustrations depicting human couples engaged in the act, it becomes more outrageous. It breaks the law which prohibits public exposure of the private parts of the body, and makes the "actors" look like dogs deprived of a sense of shame. It provokes untimely sexual arousal in the youngsters, and drives them to unhealthy activities.

However, children are indeed influenced by the mysterious events which strike their attention and often seek to discover the secrets behind them. They see the movement of the sun, the appearance and disappearance of the moon, the swelling of the stomach of their mothers and the birth of babies. They may ask their parents questions pertaining to such events before they can get scientific answers in schools.

Although I do not subscribe to the exaggerated claim made by some psychologists according to which sexuality starts at birth and a child often experiences masturbation before his first birthday, I strongly feel that children need greater protection nowadays in view of their relatively early maturity and in view of the widespread open pornography. Yet, some of the literature designed for children's sex education is too explicit and contains indecent illustrations. Some show small kids seeing their elder siblings engaged in revolting performances, reaching elements which, in the words of a reviewer of one of these books, "no child will ever see, no matter how obliging his adolescent siblings unless he is face up between the legs of the participants".[20] The moral damage that can be caused by the availability of such literature to children need not be emphasized.

What is really needed is a set of some guidelines for parents who are to satisfy the curiosity of their children and may be faced with some delicate questions such as those pertaining to the mechanical process of impregnation. In this respect, I venture to propose the following guidelines:

1. Answer the child's inquiry positively and kindly; neither negatively nor resentfully.

2. Instill in the child's mind the unbound power of God Who creates everything and can do anything, thus preparing him to accept incomplete answers to some of his enquiries when things are referred to God.

3. Teach the child the story of Adam and Eve, in such a simple form as to appear to be a prototype of the reproductive family pattern.

4. Pleasantly defer delicate questions when they are immaturely raised. Just tell him that he will learn the answer when he grows a little more, or when he goes to school.

---

[20]*The New York Times Book Review*, (July 13, 1975), p. 3.

5. Seek to develop in the children a deep sense of responsible awareness of God and a keen desire to observe His moral religious code.

This, I feel, should be the regular attitude of the parents. They should inspire the child with the presence of God Who always watches over us and records whatever we may do, and the necessity that we should follow all His teachings, whether they pertain to respect of other people's rights or to keeping chaste, avoiding forbidden mixing and illegitimate acts. They should be warned against the evil practices prevailing in certain societies, because of which humanity is now bleeding and a dangerous threat is posed to mankind. Exploitation of sex and open publicity of love scenes should be checked. These are very undignified and dehumanizing, and reduce the couple to low animal standards and worse. However, if a child is caught committing a minor undesirable behavior privately, he or she should not be treated with severity, lest a guilt-complex should develop. A forgiving advice will be more effective. Moreover, overly harsh discipline is harmful and is scorned by Islam.

Polygamy:

Some social scientists ventured to reconstruct a "history" of marriage. They claimed that man was first promiscuous, then improved by adopting a "group marriage" system in which a limited number of men shared the sexual favors of a limited number of women. Then, they say, further improvements were made over stages in which the number of the spouses on either side or both was limited until the number was reduced to one on each side; and thus monogamy in which only one woman and one man were exclusively committed in the nuptial bond has become the optimum superior pattern of marriage. This approach is now abandoned by the more serious scientists, as no valid evidence could be brought forward to substantiate this pseudo-historical story.[21]

---

[21]In our own view, marriage was regulated by God through the teachings of His Messengers. Only when their missions were forgotten or corrupted, did abuses occur.

Social scientists apply the term "polygamy" both to the practice in which a woman is married to more than one husband, precisely called "polyandry", and to the more frequent practice in which a man is married to more than one wife, which they call "polygyny". I use the term polygamy above in the latter sense.

Early human society realized the danger inherent in the practice of polyandry, and it was therefore rarely applied. The danger lay not only in the severe competition that would arise between jealous husbands but mainly in the confusion over determining the paternity of the children. That confusion does not arise in the practice of polygyny. It also seems that the interruption of the female sexual capacity during the monthly and postnatal menstrual periods and the lack of such interruption in males had something to do with the greater frequency of polygyny.

Under the influence of the writing of early European travelers who tended to publicize exotic cultural phenomena unfamiliar at home, the practice of polygamy, though rare among Muslims, became one of the features best known about Islam in the West, where its meaning and significance in its context was lost and misunderstood.

Islam, it is true, permits a restricted type of polygyny, but does not encourage it. Under no circumstances is a husband permitted to have five or more wives, which had not been uncommon before and at the time of the rise of Islam. And marrying more than one wife has always been conditional upon the anticipation of a faithful application of the principle of justice between the co-wives. The husband's time and attention must be truly shared, and any gesture or action that might provoke the jealousy of a wife must be avoided. If the husband of two wives were to go on a journey, he had to take them both with him or leave them both at home. If he could take one only, she was to be chosen by drawing lots. The next journey was to be the other's turn. The Koran eloquently stresses this duty by warning the husband contemplating another marriage in the following terms:

"But if you should fear that you will not do justice, then confine yourself to one wife." KORAN IV, 3.

It is to be borne in mind, however, that this liberal legislation was made against a restrictive background of psychological, social and economic factors. The human inclination normally confines a man to mating with one spouse; and the fear of the tension at home which is bound to arise from bringing in a co-wife, and the financial burden involved, are safeguards against uncontrolled frequency of polygyny. Moreover, the Koran guards against the abuse of this liberalism by warning:

"And indeed you cannot do justice between women, even when you are eager to be [completely just]. KORAN IV, 129.

This Islamic liberal legislation, combined with the restrictive social and natural factors, as well as the stress on the principle of justice between co-wives, which is difficult to apply, has produced a limited and balanced flexibility which has provided healthy outlets in compelling situations in which a husband has to take another wife but cannot part with the first one out of compassion or for other reasons. Traditional pressures and the sterility of the first wife were the most frequent factors leading to polygyny, which has been the rare exception.

An important point which has to be made clear in this context is that Islam gives the state the right to legislate rules which may at some point of time narrow down the degree of permissibility granted by the faith in the interest of society. No one questions the government's right to limit driving to one side of the road, or to forbid parking in certain places, or to prohibit the import or export of certain items, or building above a certain height. In the same way the legislature of a state may, if it is in the interest of its people, enact a law forbidding bigamy, a law which may be repealed after a war resulting in an excessive surplus of women, to protect them from descending to the most degrading profession.

Divorce:

During the last few years, it has been repeatedly claimed in the American press that divorce in Islam is effected by the husband's saying to his wife: "I divorce thee" three times.

The implication is that Islamic divorce is too easy, that the Muslim family is unstable and that women are ill treated and that a wife is living always under the fear of being arbitrarily and unilaterally abandoned by her husband at his whim.

This is a case of over-simplification and misleading misrepresentation. The procedure of divorce may appear to be less complicated; but simplicity of procedure does not mean that the action involved is taken lightly. The Islamic procedure of the marriage contract itself may appear to be easy and simple, yet it entails deep commitments and serious responsibilities. Similarly divorce involves moral, financial, psychological, spiritual, legal and social consequences, and therefore it cannot be taken lightly no matter how simple its procedure might seem to be.

In an Islamic setting, marriage is almost universally stable. As observed earlier, the marriage tie is regarded as a legal link and a sacred bond reinforced by mutual love and tender sentiments which grow in depth and magnitude with time and is further intensified by the birth of children. When tension arises at home, the couple, under social and religious pressure, struggle to maintain that bond. Even when tension intensifies, they are strongly recommended to seek to make peace, unyielding to anger, and to forgive each other. They should not contemplate divorce hastily. The Prophet warned:

"Among all permissible things, divorce is the most hated act to God."[22]

He also said:

"Divorce causes the Throne of God to shake."[23]

an eloquent metaphor denoting the degree of God's displeasure when a divorce takes place without sufficient grounds. He also said:

---

[22]Ibn Majah, *Sunan*, I, 650.
[23]Al-Sha'rani, *op. cit.*, 82.

"A wife who asks for divorce without legitimate reasons
will never taste the smell of Paradise."[24]

Should the atmosphere at home become tense and disputes
become chronic, the couple are advised to seek reconciliation
through the intervention of arbiters representing each side.
The Koran reads:

"And if you fear a breach between the two, appoint an
arbiter from his people and an arbiter from her people. If
they both desire agreement, God will effect harmony
between them."KORAN IV, 35

The arbiters should try to reconcile the couple to each other.
They are to conduct the case discreetly to avoid embarassment
that may arise from the publicity involving private details.
That is why each is to be from among the people of each party
of the couple, or at least should enjoy his or her trust and confidence. The arbiters' ruling should be binding, and if
necessary, enforced by the court. If the arbiters fail to reconcile the couple, divorce may become then the inevitable
necessary evil, a last resort in the interest of both parties.

We hardly need to emphasize that the above procedure, in addition to religious disapproval and the social stigma attached
to divorcees, has worked against hasty divorces.

We may add here that although the husband used to have
greater power in deciding a divorce, a woman has always had
the right to add in the marriage contract a term granting her
equal power to divorce her husband. Even without that
provision she has always had the right to seek a divorce on
certain grounds such as cruelty and the failure by the husband
to provide her with maintenance. There is nowadays a growing
tendency in Islamic countries to make divorce a state matter so
that a couple contemplating divorce has to apply for it in
court. This would be a further protection against hasty divorces. Another measure against hasty divorce is the prohibition
under the Islamic law, of divorce during the period of the

[24]Ibn Majah, *Ibid.*, II, 662.

wife's menstruation and during a clear period in which coitus took place.

A feature of the Islamic divorce is that it does not require a separation or a waiting period prior to divorce, although a waiting period of about three months is imposed on the divorced woman before she can remarry in order to determine the paternity of her child in case she is pregnant. If she is pregnant at the time of divorce, her waiting period is the remaining part of pregnancy. Otherwise, the period of waiting is three months from the time of divorce. In the case of menstruating women, the waiting period comes to an end when the second menstruation after the divorce has ceased.

Speaking of marriage reconciliation, one may see the advantages of the Koranic way of reconciling disputing couples through arbiters over the currently popular use of the services of psychotherapists and marriage counselors. The arbiters are persons to whom the welfare of the parties is of great concern. Resort to a professional counsellor who is naturally interested in his fees, is a practice that does not appeal to us. The practitioner is a stranger from whom the private life of the couple should be withheld. This rule should be particularly observed in the case of the couple's sexual relationship, being the most intimate and private aspect of their life.

Yet, in order to promote their business some professional marriage counselors propagate the idea which regards unsatisfactory sex as the pivotal factor for almost all marital misunderstandings and maintain that most causes of domestic disputes could be removed by sex therapy. Some have abused the practice by introducing most unhealthy "therapeutic" methods including "group sex" sessions, and swinging spouses. Some, if not many, God knows, may take advantage of their victims. Cases of such appalling violations have surfaced in the press recently. One is confused by the court's treatment of these cases, trying the practitioner alone and only for malpractice, not for adultery. I also feel the "patient" should be brought to task for cooperating with the practitioner on account of their mutual offence. The "victim" in a recent case, instead, was awarded one quarter and one tenth of one million dollars! She was single, but she had gone to the sex therapist seeking relief from depression.

To us, the therapy for depression and all crisis situations is to fall back to God, remembering His favors meditating and reflecting on the marvels of His creations, silently or engaging our tongue in praise of God's name or the recitation of His sacred words. And we seek marital reconciliation directly through trusted arbiters who maintain the privacy of the couple, protecting their honor and the good name of their families.

Common Law Marriage:

Common law marriage means that a man and a woman agree to live together, without a contract or an officiant. This type of marriage is a Western phenomenon. Although it was stopped in some European countries and in many states of the U.S.A., some of the American states still recognize it. Where this marriage pattern is considered legal, children resulting from it are regarded as legitimate, and the bond entails inheritance and all other rights and obligations arising from the regular type of marriage.

The question now is whether this common law marriage is legitimate in Islam. Obviously it is not, since the Islamic law insists, for marriage to be legally valid, on a solemn contract in which one party offers herself or himself categorically in marriage and the other party responds indicating acceptance of this offer in marriage, and that this unambiguous exchange should be in the presence of at least two credited witnesses.

The Islamic marriage contract in its simple form resembles the common law marriage in that it does not need an officiant or a marriage license. Yet a marriage without a license might lead to legal difficulties, pertaining to the couple, to their children and to their relatives. And Islam urges the state to introduce legislation regulating the activities and interactions of its citizens as may be deemed to be in their best interests. Nowadays, governments of all Islamic countries have adopted regulatory marriage laws; and in the United States a marrying couple must obtain a marriage license from the competent local authorities. The form of the license, its wording, its contents and its duration vary from state to state. However, a license authorizes the officiating person, a clergyman or otherwise, to conduct the ceremony of the marriage contract.

Members of the Islamic faith are urged never to marry without a license. This advice is particularly addressed to women. It is certainly a measure taken to protect their interests. The man who deceives a woman to marry him without a license is disobedient, because he thereby violates an Islamic teaching according to which a citizen has to comply with the law of his state. He very likely intends to exploit the woman to his own advantage, and without a marriage license or official registration he can commit concealed bigamy.

Birth Control:

Birth control is a deliberate measure whereby fertilization of the human egg is obstructed, thereby reducing the frequency of birth to the desired number of children. Many methods are now used to prevent conception, from interrupting coitus at the moment of male ejaculation, to surgical sterilization of either party of the couple. Though the Pill and IUD may be proven statistically effective in the prevention of birth, they are said to have some dangerous side effects which outweigh their initial value. The question which concerns us is whether the exercise of these measures of birth control is permissible under the law of Islam.

There can be no dispute over two facts: One is that the practice of birth control, unless called for by legitimate causes, conflicts with the Islamic virtue of relying upon God and trusting in Him. It also disagrees with the desirability of increasing the number of the members of the human race. The other fact is that surgical sterilization should certainly be prohibited, unless medically required. It is mutilation of the human body, and its aim conflicts with the purpose of divine creation.

In the past only one method of birth control was known; namely, withdrawal at the time of ejaculation so that no drop of semen could be deposited in the vaginal passage. Ancient people could see, even before the development of science, a connection between coitus and the incidence of pregnancy, and thus conceived of that method in which the fertilizing matter is neutralized. This practice was in fact current among the Arabs at the time of the Prophet and he was actually asked about it. Permission was granted, but the answer was given in sour terms, which implied a sense of undesirability.

Some scholars maintain that all methods of birth control are forbidden, arguing that any practice of birth control amounts to infanticide, and the Koran teaches:

"Kill not your children for fear of poverty. We shall provide sustenance for them as well as for you." KORAN XVII, 31.

Along with many others, I disagree with this exaggerated view. As we know, lawful fertilization of the ovum depends upon a number of steps, none of which is a mandatory obligation. These include marriage, intercourse, and continuation of it till ejaculation. Moreover, masturbation, which is a deliberate waste of the fertilizing force, is said to be permissible when fornication is otherwise feared, according to some jurists. General prohibition conflicts with these realities.

To summarise we may say that the practice of birth control, apart from the surgical sterilization method, is permissible, though undesirable, subject to certain conditions. Both parties, husband and wife, should mutually agree to it. Moreover, the method they adopt should not entail a physical or psychological damage to either party. In addition, their intention should be legitimate. In short, the practice of birth control may be tolerated in special circumstances, depending on the private conditions of a couple and their intention; but it should not be made the general policy of a Muslim society.

Abortion:

Unlike birth control, abortion means the elimination of an already fertilized living human entity; and a deliberate abortion with no justifiable grounds is regarded as a murderous crime. Only when the continuation of pregnancy constitutes a real threat to the life of the expectant mother is abortion permitted. Then, instead of losing two lives we are saving the fuller and already grown life of the mother.

A few jurists, however, make a difference between an abortion during the early four months of pregnancy and an abortion performed during the later period. They believe that the fetus during the first one-hundred-and-twenty days of its existence is not a full human life yet. They argue on the basis of a *hadith* which describes the stages of the formation of the fetus in the womb of its mother. According to this *hadith*, "the spirit (or the soul) is blown into the fetus" one-hundred-and-forty days after conception. Therefore they feel that the destruction of a fetus during that early stage, though most undesirable except for medical reasons, is not a serious sin if it is done safely.

The argument of these few jurists, permitting abortion in the early stage of pregnancy, does not seem to be quite agreeable. The text they quote, and on the basis of which they argue, was not meant to offer a scientific biological explanation of fetal development, on which a legal argument could rest. It was rather an eloquent theological metaphor, expressing the overwhelming power of God and the amazing subtleties of His creation and the great debt we owe Him. When it spoke of blowing a spirit into that morsel of flesh, it did not mean to denote a sharp line dividing the fetal life into two categories, one in which the fetus is a vegetable and the other a human being. In other words, the *hadith* should not be taken literally; and abortion is thus a strictly forbidden practice at any stage unless the survival of the expectant mother is threatened by the continuation of her pregnancy, as stated above.

CHAPTER VII
LIBERATION OF WOMEN

Prejudices Against Women:

We believe in women's birthright to equality with men. Owing to certain natural differences the domestic functions and obligations of women have to be different from, but reciprocal and complementary to those of men.

We believe that this framework of equality between men and women, with reciprocal complementary functions, as expounded earlier in this work, was the condition which had prevailed in human society from the time of the beginning of human life and continued as such for the most part of man's long existence on earth until prejudices and discrimination against women began to assert themselves. This belief is sustained by anthropological findings resulting from the study of surviving primitive societies which have preserved some considerable degree of the original sex equality.

It seems that prejudices against women started in "civilized" societies when the need for the woman's labor became less, and greater importance was attached to male children for their greater economic value. Worse prejudices struck deep roots when man began to build up kingdoms and vast empires based on military conquests which called for the promotion of the masculine ferocious qualities and condemned the gentle femininity as timidity, meanness and cowardice. The virile features of prowess, aggressiveness, strength and fearlessness were praised and sung as noble and generous virtues; whereas the softer, sympathetic tendencies were criticized as ugly, feminine-like and shameful weaknesses. Women became helpless, and gradually succumbed to their humiliating role as receptacles of human reproduction and servants to their male masters. They had to accept and internalize painful norms and values which sanctioned their oppression and consolidated their servile status. The insecure woman idolized her hero, the man on whom she depended; she sang his praise, sought to win his attention and craved to fulfill his wishes which centered on the satisfaction of his sensual avarices and the birth of coveted male children. Traces of this attitude can be detected in many situations. In some social settings, for example, a boy who commits an error may be reproached by his angry teacher or trainer, even in the presence of women-folk including his mother and sisters with such insults as "O you woman!" or, "You are nothing but a woman!"Or, "This error can be done only by a woman!" The women present in these social settings listen to these insults in good humor and do not seem to feel offended.

To those oppressive men, women symbolized the weak vices they hated because they were unsuited to the quest for conquest and exploitation: namely, fear and cowardice. Women were even used as scapegoats when severe setbacks or defeat were suffered, and were therefore condemned as bad omens and the source of all evils or the evil itself. And when a conquest was achieved and the vanquished were enslaved, the male bondsmen were used in building monuments which brought glory to the conquerers and perpetuated their names, whereas the slave women were relegated to the more un-dignifying pursuit of satisfying the animal instincts of their oppressors. In using these tender creatures for their insatiable sensual desires, these virile masters subjected them to sadistic tortures and savage punishment, deriving greater pleasure from their painful appeals for mercy and the sound of their moaning complaints. They humiliated them in their public gatherings by compelling them to expose their naked flesh in exciting obscene dancing movements which sharpened their own appetite and fed their devouring eyes, thus reinforcing more deeply the females' low position in society.

Virtuous women sought to protect their honor in seclusion voluntarily or under duress from their jealous male masters; and the practice of women's segregation was gradually and in-creasingly institutionalized, especially among classes of

nobility. The segregated women confined themselves to their homes, and assumed a heavy cover when they were exposed to the public eye.

Further discussion of this interesting theme of discrimination against women, its roots, its development and its manifestations would be beyond the scope of this work. The above observations sufficiently demonstrate the prejudicial conditions which, prior to the rise of Islam, prevailed in all the so-called "civilized societies", though in varying degrees. Societies less civilized, like the pre-Islamic Arab tribes, developed an ambivalent attitude of female humiliation and female glorification. They practiced female infanticide, but some women of their nobility could attain social prominence. But societies which espoused a rigid patriarchal system looked upon their women as liabilities or mere parasites tolerated for their reproductive and recreational value!

What is more regrettable was that the women's misfortunes were confirmed by religious beliefs which absorbed these prejudices, internalized them further and gave them a religious sanction. Unfortunately, this is true of Eastern and Western religions, those which claim a heavenly revelation and those which do not.[1] We believe, however, that these prejudices said to exist in Christianity and Judaism did not belong to the original teachings of these great faiths and cannot claim a divine origin. God is the Lord of justice. We cannot imagine that He may be prejudiced against the gentle half of His creatures.

What Has Islam Done For Women?

Islam, which appeared fourteen centuries ago, simply and effectively restored the birthright of women to equality with men. It extirpated the old prejudices against women. It exonerated Eve from the responsibility of Adam's fall. The Koran tells us that both Eve and Adam were equally under the

---

[1]See, for example, David and Vera Mace, *Marriage East and West,* Doubleday and Co., Inc. 1960, pp. 60ff, and *Encyclopedia of Religion and Ethics,* V, p. 271b.

divine order not to eat from a certain tree. It also tells that they both were seduced by Satan. They both sinned. They were both equally blamed and expelled from the Garden. And they together repented unto God. Let us listen to their story in the words of the Koran:

> " 'Adam! Dwell with your wife in the Garden, and enjoy its good things as you wish; but approach not this tree, or you run into harm and transgression.' Then began Satan to whisper suggestions to them in order to bring openly before their minds all their shame that had been hidden from them. He said: 'Your Lord only forbade you this tree lest you should become angels or such beings as live forever.' And he swore to them that he was advising them sincerely. So by deceit he brought about their fall. When they tasted of the tree their shame became manifest to them and they began to sew together the leaves of the Garden over their bodies. And their Lord called unto them: 'Did I not forbid you both that tree, and tell you both that Satan was an avowed enemy unto you?' They said, 'Our Lord! We have wronged our own souls. If You forgive us not and bestow not upon us Your Mercy, surely we shall be among the losers!' "

> KORAN VII, vv. 19-23
> (Cf. II, 35-37; and XX, 115-122)

Under the law of Islam, as explained earlier, a woman, like a man, is a responsible free agent, fully entitled to all civil rights, and is to be treated with dignity and respect. When she is under age, she is to be taken good care of and never to be subjected to ill treatment on account of her sex. Her right to a good education is established, like that of her brother. Taking good care of a girl is particularly emphasized and promised great rewards.

When a girl becomes of age, her independence is fully recognized. Her character is never absorbed in that of her father or in that of her husband. A Muslim woman, single or married, has one name and a perpetual personality. She does not adopt her husband's name on marriage. Her legal independent status is permanent. Married or single, she can enter into contracts, conduct business, own property and dispose of her wealth at will, maintain and operate separate bank accounts, and may loan and borrow under her own name. She is under the same moral and religious obligations, is urged to cultivate her talents and utilize her potentialities in her best interest. She is not to be coerced into a marriage she does not care for, and her consent to a marriage proposal is crucial. She is entitled to full and equal rewards for her labor, and it would be an injustice to treat her otherwise. Past prejudices against women, which went so far as to include burying female infants alive, wife abuse, and the inheritance of a man's widow with no regard for her wishes, were condemned and stopped. Marriage was regulated on a fair legal basis, and the conjugal relationship was organized in such a way as to promote harmony and happiness, and as to provide for efficient smooth fulfillment of the spouses. Islam also established the woman's right to inheritance as a daughter of the deceased person, or as his mother, his sister or his widow. It also gave her a right to the payment of a dowery on marriage by her groom, which is symbolic of respect for her and indicative of winning her through voluntary consent, not through compulsion or abduction as was the case in some societies. The ancient Arabs used to sing poems in pride of winning their brides by the sword. In the light of the above, fair-minded writers regard Islam and its Prophet as the true liberator of women.

In certain areas, however, Islam has allowed some differences in certain rights and responsibilities of men and women, consistent with their different biological and psychological makeup. Reference to some of these differences was made earlier, but let us recapitulate them here in the context of women's liberation.

Under the law of Islam, a woman is granted relief of certain religious duties such as prayers and fasting during the postnatal period and the period of menstruation. During pilgrimage in Mecca, while a man discards his regular clothes for two unseamed pieces of cloth wrapped around his body, a woman maintains her regular full dress leaving only her face and the palms of her hands uncovered. These religious exemptions which are obviously consistent with the women's female nature and needs are adequate reliefs, not prejudiced inequality.

Maintenance of the wife, even when she is earning, is the responsibility of her husband. A divorced wife is also entitled to her support during the waiting period she has to observe before she becomes entitled to remarry in order to determine whether she is pregnant or not, and in order not to confuse the fatherhood of her baby if she should be pregnant. The maintenance of her children under her custody and the cost of their education is also the duty of their father. Again this is not a harmful inequality or an insult to the woman. To make a wife legally responsible for her own maintenance would be an unfair burden on women, many of whom may not be able to afford it. It may also undermine the chances of marital success and domestic harmony. To make her, with her husband, equally responsible for the cost of the household would very likely lead to harmful disputes and chronic misunderstandings. Misunderstandings over financial matters seem to be responsible for most domestic upheavals. If the wife is left to volunteer any share of the cost of the household under no compulsion, room for disputes and quarrels would be reduced. In fact, her voluntary help would promote a better relationship.

It was also remarked earlier in this work that man should be the head of the household, the captain who formulates its policy. This does not mean that he should do so alone, or behave arbitrarily or tyrannically. It does not imply superiority or greater merit. It should be a loving sympathetic authority, and a cooperative and shared responsibility. This conjugal "authority", which is consistent with the rule which says: "Who pays controls", should be benevolent and considerate and should fully recognize the dignity of the wife and her right to be treated as an equal partner. Within this prescribed framework, however, the couple builds their own pattern of relationship based upon their personal moods, inclinations, likes and dislikes. This pattern eventually assumes a spectrum of attitudes and responses, so that when an attitude is assumed by either in a situation, or when something occurs and either reacts in a special way, it arouses a response by the other party often agreeable to the first party. The function of this general prescribed framework of conjugal relationship is to delineate to the couple the basic outlines which should guide them in their effort to build their own pattern, making compromises and adaptations. Each party of the couple would know his or her own limits, which can be invoked in the case of disagreement. Couples are thus at liberty to structure the pattern of their special relationship as may best suit them and assure their mutual satisfaction and fulfillment.

Unlike some other systems which deny women or some categories of women a right in the estate of deceased close relatives, Islam recognizes the right of inheritance to all surviving daughters of the deceased person, his or her mother, his widow and all his surviving sisters.

Critics, however, blame the law which makes the share of the inheriting sister half that of her inheriting brother. Yet, the alternative, which is to entitle them to equal shares would be inconsistent with the needs of each. The brother is a husband and a father, actually or potentially. As such, he is in charge of a family and is responsible for their needs and the cost of their living, in addition to the cost of his own needs. His sister, on the other hand, is relieved from all these burdens. Even her own cost of living is the duty of someone else. To grant her half the share of her brother when they inherit together either as a son and daughter or as a brother and sister of the deceased person is more consistent with that law.

The position of women as outlined above, asserting their equitable status, guaranteeing their civic, legal and moral rights and prescribing a pattern of reciprocal rights and obligations based upon their functional differences, strikes a fair working balance which can operate smoothly and efficiently and lead to social equilibrium and personal fulfillment.

Need for Women's Liberation in Modern Times:

The Islamic reforms were operative only among nations and communities which adopted that faith. Outside that purview, the old prejudices against women and their exploitation persisted until recent times. Although the manifestations of these prejudices assumed a variety of ways of ill treatment and different degrees of oppression, the suppression of women was a universal common factor.

Even the reforms brought about by Islam had to react to, and interact with remnants of ancient prejudices particularly in moral and social treatment, especially in societies where the coming of Islam had been preceded by a civilization based on military conquest and the virile qualities of man. Thus, the ancient powers which had arisen prior to the coming of Islam and which were absorbed into its nascent state during its early decades and whose people were destined to play an effective role in the political and cultural life of Islam, brought to Muslim societies some of their old prejudices against women. Apparently, their severe segregation system appealed to the Islamic call upon women to observe a greater degree of modesty and to cover their attractions when they were exposed to the public eye. In due course, the custom of assuming a heavy veil by women and their seclusion became institutionalized, especially among the nobility and the higher classes. Events from the third century of Islam under the caliphate of Baghdad seem to have played a part in this direction. The wealth, leisure and the growing sensuality and immoral pursuits of royalty, their courtiers and wealthy merchants, and the abuse and misuse of female slaves who were brought in large numbers from all parts of the world, provoked unbearable jealousies among men and stirred deep fears over the chastity of their own women. These conditions did not only condone acceptance of ancient segregation customs but seem to have intensified them and given them a cause for sanction. Heavy segregation of women and negligence of their rights became an almost universal feature in the world of Islam, although their legal rights could not be denied.

Recent pressures from the West and the relative instability caused by rapid changes have brought about a great deal of confusion in some Muslim societies, especially since the turn of the twentieth century. Modern education was first resented for its missionary tinge; but when it was adopted for its economic and prestigious advantages it was denied to the female half of the nation. After all, the destiny of the girl was to get married. Her education did not seem to enhance her marriage chances. In fact, educated women were somewhat feared and even mistrusted. When literate, they could communicate and romanticise secretly with men. Educated women were thought to be obtrusive and too assertive, and they did not seem to appeal to men who expected them to serve them and obey them blindly. Parents, or rather the fathers, refused to allow their daughters to go to school. The Islamic ideals pertaining to education became some how confused. Moreover, going out to school was inconsistent with the ideal of women's segregation. When a girl reached the age of adolescence, she was to stay at home and not to be seen by strange men. Even the mention of the name of one's wife or a female relative was embarrassing. We heard of some communities in which women's segregation was so severe that small girls who could not be restrained from stepping out of their home were dressed in boy's clothes so that they could not be recognized in public as girls. Even the coffin of a dead woman was not to be seen by a strange man. When a woman died, she was hurriedly buried by her close relatives before the news could reach the ears of sympathizers who might come home to offer their condolences before the burial. That shows how far local customs were removed from the genuine teachings of the faith and the practice of the Prophet.

The result was that the Muslim woman, in many cases, was a victim of ignorance and severe oppression. She did not know her rights under the law. She did not know that she had a legal right to choose her life partner. She did not know, and may not know now, that she was entitled to stipulate in her marriage contract a right to divorce her husband at will, or that she should be informed of her husband's intention should he decide in the future to become polygamous, in which case she might seek divorce from him.

Furthermore, with urbanization in recent decades and the relative release from traditional social pressures, it became easier for men to abuse their privileges. They ill-treated their wives, exaggerating the degree granted to men over them. They divorced them haphazardly and some committed polygamy irresponsibly, oblivious to the misfortunes to be suffered by the first wife. In some cases, the law, or rather its misuse, led to greater confusion. In Egypt, for example, a humiliating institution called "The House of Obedience" was developed and incorporated in the law in 1897.

According to this law, a wife who absconded from the conjugal domicile could be forced to return to it by the court. In case she had reasons to refuse to go to the same house, the husband was required to provide another dwelling. The angry husband, who had no real intention to make peace with his alienated wife, often chose an oppressive dwelling in which the wife would suffer terrible isolation or torture from hostile neighbors. If she refused to go, out of fear, she was dragged by the police like a criminal and locked inside her room! Although the practice was rarely resorted to, it has been regarded by the Egyptian feminists as a symbol of female humiliation. The demand of its revocation is now on the top of the list of their program for reform.

In summary, the need for adequate reforms to liberate women and restore them to their legitimate rights in the modern age became a cause of universal importance—in Eastern, Western and Islamic societies.

Women's Liberation Movements in Western Society:

With the revolutionary trends in the modern age, leading to profound reforms in the various aspects of life, women were awakened to their rights and became conscious of their misfortune and the artificial barriers in the way of their liberty. This consciousness led to the rise of feminist movements for liberation. The most vigorous among them was that which developed in the West. My particular interest in this movement, is mainly because of its repercussions on women in the Muslim world and on my own Muslim sisters living in Western society. I am particularly interested in its manifestations, rather than its history.

The reason for the fact that the Western liberation movement of women was more vigorous and more glamorous than its counterparts elsewhere is not difficult to seek. The Western woman was laboring under greater burdens of suppression and prejudices and legal incapacities inherited from a prejudicial past, perpetrated and sanctioned by myth, religion and deeply-rooted social customs. In an essay written just a little over a century ago on the subjugation of women, John Stuart Mill tells us of the distressing conditions of women in his time, and how men enslaved their women physically and mentally. He described in vivid terms how women were led to believe that the ideal character of the female was "complete self-negation and full submission to their men: no self-will or even self-control".

About a century earlier, a British lawyer defined the legal status of a wife in the following terms:

> "By marriage, the husband and wife are one person in law; that is, *the very being or legal existence of the woman is suspended during marriage,* or at least is incorporated and consolidated into that of the husband . . . But though our laws in general consider man and wife as one person, yet there are instances in which she is separately considered as *an inferior to him, and acting by his compulsion.'*[2]

In spite of a series of spectacular reforms enacted in Europe and the U.S.A. during the second half of the 19th century and the early part of the current century, promoted by a better climate created by the work of such thinkers as John Stuart Mill and the writing of female leaders, as well as by the pressure of the vigorous feminist movements which occasionally resorted to violent means, traces of the past prejudices and discrimination still remained. The harsh subjugation of women for far too long under the ancient patriarchal system left deep scars in the mind of the Western woman, and mutual suspicion and fear between the sexes still survived. Feminist activism which remained dormant in Western countries since its glamorous successes in the 1920's, having suffered severe eclipses in Germany and the Soviet Union during the 1930's, has been vigorously reawakened since the 1960's, aligning itself to youth revolt and to civil rights' movements.

---

[2]Blackstone's *Commentary,* vol. I, "Rights of Persons", 3rd Ed., 1768 p. 44.

We should not therefore be deceived by the apparent good materialistic condition of the Western woman and by the superficial courtesy extended to her in public by her male partner. Until the recent past, the Western woman was under severe legal incapacities related to financial transactions and property ownership. In some instances, her labor is until now less rewarded than that of her male counterpart. Her domestic role as a housekeeper and a children's nurse was thought to be so rigidly fixed as not to allow modification. Her legitimate ambition to recover her rights and participate in public life was rigidly opposed and deeply resented by men. Urban life brought about isolation, impersonalization and further alienation. The reaction was commensurately violent.

The success of the women's liberation movement was not even in all the Western nations. In the American setting, which is of greater interest to us, women have been able to remove many of the obstacles which had been in the way of their self-fulfillment. Additional enactments have been made in recent years, asserting women's equal rights in education, health and in public life. Yet, they are still struggling for greater gains.

The latest legal reform is a constitutional amendment known as the Equal Rights Amendment, which states that:

> "Equality of rights under the law shall not be denied by the United States or by any state on account of sex."

This amendment, which was passed by the Congress in 1972, needs to be ratified by the legislatures of 38 states by March 1979 in order to become a law. Although it was quickly ratified by 22 states in the same year, the Amendment lost momentum as quickly, and the process of its ratification which has become one of the major objectives of the various American feminist organizations led by the NOW (National Organization of Women) became slow and tortuous as the amendment soon became very controversial. It has provoked strong opposition, especially among women who deeply suspect the leadership of the feminist movement. Only eight states ratified the amendment in 1973, three did so in 1974 and one in 1975. This makes a total of 34, although the legislatures of two states, Nebraska and Tennessee have voted to rescind it. This was the result of the work of the opponents of the amendment, who are vigorously seeking to discourage the legislatures of the remaining states from voting for it. The status of the amendment has suffered another setback in the states of New York and New Jersey, which had ratified the Federal Amendment in 1972. The electorates of these two states in November 1975 stunned the feminists by rejecting their state equal rights amendments, which resembled the Federal ERA.

The grievances against the amendment are summed up by Phyllis Schlafly, a leading opponent to the amendment who speaks of marriage and family as "my No. 1 career", in the following words:

> "It won't do anything to help women, and it will take
> away from women the rights they already have, such as
> the right of a wife to be supported by her husband, the
> right of a woman to be exempted from military combat,
> and your right, if you wanted it, to go to a single sex
> college."[3]

Other opponents denounce the amendment as anti-marriage and anti-family and fear that it might lead to unisex toilets. Under the proposed law, they say, divorced women would lose their almost automatic right to child custody and those with income would lose their right to alimony.

Mrs. Schlafly, in denouncing the ERA adds:

> "It won't give women any rights in employment or
> education or in credit, because those rights are already
> there in the Equal Opportunity Act of 1972, the
> education amendments of 1972, and the Equal Credit
> Opportunity Act of 1974."[4]

On account of some extremist views held by some elements in the feminist movement, Mrs. Schlafly, who is said to be of

---

[3]Judy Klemesrud, "Opponents of E.R.A. Confident of Its Defeat" *The New York Times*, (December 15, 1974) p. 44.
[4]*Ibid.*

a wide experience, a well-established author and is described as an immaculately groomed woman, echoes the position of many American women toward that movement when she describes it as:

> "An anti-family movement that is trying to make perversion acceptable as an alternative life-style. Most women find their major fulfillment in the home. In my scale of values, home, family and husband come first, and I think that's the way most people feel."[5]

Whether the Equal Rights Amendment will be ratified or otherwise, we hope that there will be no serious conflict with the basic parts of our family law which we, as Muslims living in America, prefer to follow. We do not like our wives or daughters to be deprived of their rights of maintenance or alimony. We do not wish our law of inheritance to be affected, or to see ourselves compelled to abandon our law of personal status for the namesake of equality when it entails inequity.

Liberation of the Muslim Woman:

Feminist movements also started in the Islamic countries, calling for the improvement of the status of women in society. Ironically, these movements started first at the hands of men who called for reforms in all walks of life, like Muhammad Abduh and Qasim Amin who flourished in Egypt in the latter part of the preceding century. The latter man particularly devoted much of his energy to the cause of women's liberation, though his views at the time met with resistance. Women later continued these efforts forming their own organizations since the early part of this current century.

The call of these early reformers was for girl's education and for the relaxation of the practice of women's segregation. They also called for a sensible control of the divorce law and for curbing the practice of polygamy. However, the feminist movement in an Islamic setting has been less dramatic and far

---

[5]*Ibid.*

less militant than its counterpart in the West. This was not merely because of lesser educational attainment by the Muslim woman but Muslim women were not really under severe legal incapacities. They may have suffered from the misapplication or the abuse of certain laws, particularly those of polygamy and divorce. Moreover, in most areas of the so-called Third World, men like women need to be liberated. In other words, women alone have fewer causes of grievance. The objectives of the women's movement in most Muslim settings have been to provide greater opportunities for the education of girls, better training of women in various areas, guidance in family planning efforts, greater participation in social welfare work and the efforts toward the realization of national goals. This, or course, is in addition to their concern over the need to improve the divorce and polygamy laws.

A typical Muslim feminist movement is one that started in Egypt. I have chosen it for the purpose of illustration as it provides inspiring features. Egypt, being the seat of al-Azhar University, the world's leading influential Islamic theological seminary, is believed to represent the most dogmatic but best scholarly, conservative type in Islam. On the other hand, due to its geographic position, Egypt has been exposed, perhaps more than any other part of the world of Islam, to foreign influences, particularly from Europe. In recent history, it was subjected to Turkish, French and British rules. As late as 1956 Egypt labored under foreign occupation. The French conquest, though brief, was of far-reaching cultural influence. The interaction between the traditional "conservative" forces, which have an effective role of influence over the whole world of Islam, on the one hand, and the modernist forces converging not only from Western capitalism, but also, especially in recent years, from Eastern socialism, results in a pattern that provides a guidance for understanding the situation in other parts which for the most part are very similar. Islam has deeply instilled in the souls of its adherents everywhere the same set of values, the same attitudes and the same ideals.

The earliest call for the cause of women's liberation, as remarked earlier, came from men who lived in the latter part of the 19th century and who sought to reform the general life style in Egypt in such a way as to suit the demands of the modern climate. One of these men was Rifa'ah Tahtawi, a member of the first batch of al-Azhar students selected by the Egyptian ruler to pursue further studies in France, who on their return became agents of seminating European thought in the country. One of the works of the brilliant and influential Tahtawi was a book called *The Honest Guide for Girls and Boys,* published in Cairo in 1873, in which the author strongly advocated women's education in order to make her a better companion to her husband and a better mother to her children.

The greatest reformer among all these men was Shaikh Muhammad Abduh who died in Cairo in 1905. He received his education and training solely in al-Azhar, although he was exiled later in his life to Beirut and Paris. His influence traveled far outside Egypt and far beyond the boundaries of the Arab world. The modern ideas brought through his students who came from foreign lands early in this century, led to controversies between the conservative and modernist forces in remote countries until the modernists gained the day. Shaikh Abduh also stressed the need for universal education as a means for reform and improvement. He argued against the continuity of the practice of polygamy which he regarded to be of no more advantage but actually socially dangerous. He said that the law of Islam provided for the abolition of an otherwise permissible practice in the interest of the community when it becomes harmful. He also called for the transfer of the right of divorce to the court itself, recourse to which should be made available equally to women and men.

The best well-known advocate of the women's cause was Qasim Amin, author of *The Modern Woman,* which appeared in Cairo in 1900.[6] He strongly called for the removal of the veil which he regarded as offensive and degrading for women. He laid a special emphasis on women's education, and called

---

[6]Three years earlier, he published his admirable work, *Liberation of Women*, in which he called for the education of women and the removal of their veil. He analyzed in vivid terms the then existing conjugal relationship between married couples in Egypt, particularly in upper classes, attributing the unsatisfactory condition to women's ignorance and their segregation.

for the enactment of laws on modern lines that would assure complete freedom for women. His views aroused a great controversy at the time, and he, like other reformers, was subjected to insults and abuses. However, the views of these men were admired and appreciated by later generations.

The efforts of these men paved the way for the birth of the feminist movement in Egypt early in this century, led by Lady Huda Sha'rawi, daughter of an influential wealthy political figure. Her background and strong personality lent a prestige to the movement especially in its early stages. It seems that the experience of her marriage by her father to a cousin 30 years her senior, when she was 14, of which she came to know only moments before her wedding, awakened her to the plight of the Egyptian woman and stirred her for action on behalf of her sisters. As a feminist activist, she participated in the political patriotic struggle in 1919, and led a street female demonstration protesting the continuation of the British occupation. That demonstration conveyed a significant message by telling the world that behind the veils there was intellectual awareness and a rebellious spirit bent upon the demand of universal liberty and human rights.

Huda Sha'rawi, who studied the Koran during her childhood and was well versed in the Arabic and French cultures, founded the Feminist Union in Egypt in 1923. Her most tangible achievement was the removal of the veil which used to be worn in public, particularly by women of upper and middle classes to cover the lower part of their faces. She had to set the example herself. On her return from a feminist conference held in Italy in 1923 she startled the welcoming party in Alexandria when she disembarked unveiled. Other women followed suit. The movement rallied support rapidly under her leadership and the press came to its side. Special women's magazines sprang up and became widely popular, some of which now survive and publish columns similar to the syndicated columns of Dear Abby and Ann Landers. The questions now deal with the dilemmas faced by young people torn between the old family traditions and the liberal modern trends, the problems of conjugal relations and women's fashions. The answers, even given by feminist leaders, reveal a reserved but enlightened conservatism, stemming from the dominating Islamic values. For example, they warn girls against easy dating but encourage them to seek participation in public life. The letters never reveal the type of outrageous permissiveness we occasionally read in letters addressed to the American columnists, such as incestuous practices and tolerance of bed suitors to one's own wife.

The early efforts of the Egyptian feminist movement were mainly aimed at providing greater opportunities for women's education, gaining for women the right to vote and to run for a political office and the reform of the law of the personal status governing family relations.

The educational goal could not receive any real resistence in Egypt, though it did in some more conservative countries although it has now become very popular everywhere. In 1922, only 43 girl students were enrolled in Egyptian Goverment secondary schools. In 1962, the number jumped to 100,000. The situation has steadily improved over the years. The following diagram shows a comparative analysis of the student population in Egypt during the academic session 1969/1970:[7]

	Girls	Boys	Total
Primary Schools	1,378,631	2,242,710	3,621,341
Preparatory	253,917	540,259	794,176
Secondary (General)	93,025	200,543	293,568
Secondary (Commerce)	66,508	69,020	135,528
Teachers' Training	11,350	13,725	25,075
Universities	40,014	121,503	161,517

It may be observed that although the university education has become an accepted pattern for girls, marriage is still regarded by most as the ultimate goal for them. The university is looked upon by some as a good market for picking a bride or capturing a groom; and in some cases the girl's university education is interrupted once she has accepted a marriage

[7]*Bulletin, Education Census in Arab Countries*, 1969/1970, Cairo Bibliotheque No. 1623, 1975, pp. 160 and 170.

proposal. This is particularly so when the engagement occurs early in her university experience. Otherwise, the engagement is accepted but the wedding is delayed until after the girl's graduation. In fewer cases, the wedding takes place during a long holiday and her education is continued.

In the political arena and public services, the women won the right to vote and to run for a public office in 1956 against strong opposition from some religious leaders who thought that a woman's active participation in public life would expose her to indecencies and she might hurt others by her tempting attractions. As a result of this reform, a number of women were elected to the National Assembly of the Arab Socialist Union, the only political party in Egypt, and some have been appointed as members of the Cabinet of Ministers. Women can now be found in almost all professions, and they are easily accepted, even welcomed in public life.

It is in the area of legal reforms concerning the domestic life that the feminist movement has been facing the stiffest opposition. The family relationships are still regulated in Egypt and indeed in all parts of the Muslim world in accordance with the part of Islamic law known as the law of personal status. In fact, this is the only part of that law which has remained operative. Until the British occupation, Egyptian courts like those in the other parts of the Islamic world, sought to follow the law of Islam in almost all cases, prior to European rule. Under European colonial influence, the importance of that law receded and secular enactments, influenced mainly by the Napoleonic Code, replaced it in all areas except the domain of personal status. For example, under the Ottoman rule, a commercial code was enacted in 1850, a penal code in 1858 and a maritime commerce code in 1868. The religious law, however, remained the ultimate guide in moral and social interactions.

The Islamic law was enshrined in reference works written by the original jurists and their disciples many centuries ago, and the courts in making decisions sought guidance from these reference books. In other words, the Islamic law was not cast in a set of terse articles, clauses and subclauses in the familiar legal fashion. When the Ottoman rulers introduced enactments in the various legal domains they also enacted a code for the area of personal status to operate through a special court known as the *shari'a* court, in distinction from the secular courts. In enacting the *shari'a* law, a specific legal school had to be chosen in order to avoid conflicts, and the school of their choice was that founded by Abu Hanifah, one of the leading Muslim jurists who passed away in A.D. 767. For a long time, this school remained the official legal system of Egypt. When the *shari'a* courts were abolished in 1956 and their jurisdiction was transferred to the civil courts, cases of personal status continued to be decided according to the *shari'a* law of personal status.

It is that law which the Egyptian feminists are seeking to modify in order to remove what they regard to be a cause of female grievances and humiliation. They demand the abolition of the institution of the "House of Obedience", to which an unwilling wife is dragged by the police and in which she is to be oppressively detained. They want also the divorce law to be reformed in the way proposed by Shaikh Muhammad Abduh. To confine the power of divorce to the court, to which recourse can be made equally by husband and wife, would in a way curb the frequency of divorce. Instead of the easy divorce procedure whereby divorce is effected by the husband's pronouncing the word at will, application to the court means a compulsory delay, a period of grace during which a change of mind may occur and reconciliation may take place. On the other hand, this procedure would be more compatible with the principle of equality. They also call for the abolition of the practice of polygyny. Although its incidence has become very rare, like recourse to the "House of Obedience", they regard the practice as harmful and humiliating and degrading to women. Another demand made by the feminists in Egypt pertains to the custody of the children. As explained earlier, a mother under the Islamic law has the right of her child's custody until the age of seven if a boy or nine if a girl. After that the child is given the choice to remain with his mother or to go to his father. Abu Hanifah, according to whose opinion the law operates, says that when the child reached the specified age, his custody automatically goes to the father. In the view of the Egyptian feminists this automatic transfer ignores the welfare of the child and injures the sentiments of his mother.

In the other parts of the Muslim world, each of which is seeking progress along the way as suits its people, their traditions and background, the progress of the liberation movement on behalf of women may assume different courses and may have peculiar basic or side problems. The case of Egypt represents a middle way, in which the movement is pushing slowly and patiently under a heavy weight of traditionalism and strong pressure of modernism. It is a midway course between what has been daringly achieved in Tunisia, for example, and the position in Saudi Arabia. In the case of the former, the President himself acted on behalf of women and in 1956 proclaimed the reform law which sought almost a complete sex equality. Polygyny has been abolished and divorce has become the responsibility of the court. In the latter country, the woman is just seeing the daybreak of her modern liberation.

Another example reflecting the variety of problems that may be encountered, is the case of the Indonesian/Malaysian world, in which the question of a facial veil hardly constituted a problem. The Indonesian/Malay woman does not seem to have been ever veiled. Her traditional attire is full, though charming and elegant. Yet their feminists may have greater grievances over the question of polygyny and divorce. The question of the use of contraceptives is more severely argued and resisted in some of these countries than it is in the others, but no voice is raised in favor of abortion without a medical cause.

Allowing for such differences and for an uneven progress, the outline of the feminist movement in Egypt well illustrates the basic points with which all other feminist movements have to struggle, the interaction between the opposing forces of traditionalism and modernism, and the ultimate compromise reached through patient feminist action based on cool but persistent, rational persuasion which seems to be a feature of the Muslim feminist movements, rather than severe incrimination or aggressive militancy.

The unevenness of the progress can be gathered from the

fact that while full political rights were granted the Muslim woman in Turkey in 1934, her sister in Iran won these in 1963. In Pakistan, in spite of the persistence of the heavy veil, the Muslim woman has been contributing her share to serving her country since independence and partition with India in 1948. It was in that year that the Syrian woman gained these rights. It is interesting, however, to note that royal houses sometimes initiated the efforts on behalf of women. The Royal family of Iran, for example, took the first step in removing the woman's veil. This was as early as 1935. Princess Aisha, daughter of the late Sultan and King of Morocco and sister of the present King, took the initiative of the struggle on behalf of the Moroccan woman in 1947 when she appeared un-veiled and openly spoke calling for the participation of women in public affairs. Another important point is the fact that even in countries considered as conservative, the power wielded by women, openly or behind the scenes, should not be under-estimated. It is also important to stress the fact that what has been obstructing the progress of the woman's cause in Muslim lands, wherever obstruction has been encountered, was not Islam but local traditions and customs.

Islam and the Modern Feminist Movements:

Islam, a faith which lays great emphasis on the objective of improving the quality of human life and the promotion of happy interpersonal relations, the removal of injustices and the amelioration of the misfortunes of downtrodden people, certainly sympathizes with the modern feminist movement in its call for a just treatment to women and the elimination of their legal incapacities and all prejudicial practices against them. To this degree, the modern feminist call is undoubtedly congruous with the spirit and guidance of Islam. We do not therefore see any justification for discrimination against women denying them equal rewards for their labor, or for in-sisting on the husband's approval before granting credit to his wife.

Thus we, Muslims, feel deeply sympathetic with the cause of the feminist liberation movement and its call for justice to women in all aspects. Yet, we cannot agree with certain views and objectives of some extremists in the movement which seem to have been generated by the unjustified resistance to the legitimate claims of the movement, or by the claim that a sex revolution must entail a complete break with the traditions, taboos and prohibitions of the past.

For instance, the extremists' demand for easy abortion on request and their insistence on honoring lesbianism and homosexuality as legitimate choices cannot be easily digested. We also are opposed to the attack by some activists in the movement against the institution of marriage, their call for unchecked sexual freedom, their endeavor to deglorify motherhood, and their propagation of immoral alternative life styles which are corrupt and destructive. Their angry reaction to men treating them as reproductive machines is understood, but this does not justify the extremely opposite trend of seeking alternatives to the functions of the vagina and the womb, substituting them by self-induced genital satisfaction and reproductive test tubes. Such genetical endeavors have their terrifying consequences. We are opposed to artificial insemination which is said to account for a large number of children in some countries. It is an open adultery. Efforts should aim instead at improving conjugal relations by infusing a better sense of responsibility, of greater and honest commitment between the spouses, of a better religious sentiment and true fear of God.

We also disagree to extending the wrath of some feminists against all men of the world, as if they are all prejudiced against women, and to the exaggerated use of incriminating words and statements portraying all men as hateful and oppressors. An enlightened male Muslim has no prejudice against women at all. After all, women are our daughters, our sisters, our mothers and our wives. We love our daughters as we love our sons. We love and respect our mothers and our sisters as we love our fathers and brothers. We love our wives and like them to remain angels shielding us with their gentle wings above. We only do not want them to descend too deeply in the earth and be badly tarnished by the dirty mud of the savage world of competitive, harsh struggle. We are concerned about the welfare, wellbeing and success of our daughters as much as, or even more than, we are concerned about the welfare and future success of our sons. To condemn all men of injustice and discrimination against women does not seem justified. Maybe men, in their concern over the wellbeing of their children have different concepts as to what constitutes the wellbeing for a female and that of a male. While a significant element in the concept of the female's wellbeing is perhaps to see the daughter happily married and well secure under the shield of a loving responsible husband, the financial security and independence is a more overriding factor in the case of the welfare of the son, who has to care for a wife and children. This stems from the functional biological differences.

We also disagree with the criticism leveled by some extremists against the status of a housewife. We believe it is a noble function. Although we do not oppose the idea that a woman may seek an outside gainful career so long as she maintains her dignity, especially before childbirth and after the children have grown, we reject the claim that being a housewife is a dull, boring and undignified pursuit which stifles the woman's potentialities. We are sick of hearing the teaching that sex games should be only for fun, and that birth control, abortion and artificial insemination are solely the woman's rights.

We cannot agree to the aspiration of some feminists to see women *legally* required to share with their husbands the cost of the household, thus depriving them from their right to maintenance and alimony. Such a legal provision would, I believe, restrain the relationship between the spouses and create a barrier of formalities between them. It is bound to create an atmosphere of discord and breed mistrust. It would make the domestic life look like a business partnership rather than an integrated social unit the members of which live under a reciprocal, interdependent relationship. So, let the husband remain the financially dominant figure, legally responsible for the sustenance of those who live under his shelter, and let his wife remain the gentle, angelic, love-inspiring soul, enjoying the feeling that she is legally sheltered by a strong responsible man. Let's not misinterpret this as a case of unfair inequality. What is important is harmony, personal fulfillment, justice and equity. Let the couple decide for themselves as to whether the earning wife should voluntarily contribute to the cost of the household, and in what manner and to what degree. Let her contribution be a gift of a willing volition, not a resentful compulsion resting upon a legal imposition.

We are also opposed to the call, by some, on women to assume an aggressive tough attitude. We hear about literature and school courses called "Assertiveness Training," designed to teach women and train them in the exercise of aggressiveness and even in the use of rude practices in their dealings with men.

In these training classes, women are also said to practice "refusing a request by using some techniques already familiar to other women who though unschooled in the art, are naturally talented in assertiveness".[8]

In my opinion, such practices are not in the best interest of women or the feminist cause. It is legitimate that a person, man or woman, should be able to assert his rights, but he does not need to be rude or to violate the rights of others. Training people to develop a balanced character capable of preserving its own rights in a legitimate manner should better be the responsibility of the home.

One of the promoters of the "Assertiveness" program was quoted as saying, "women are victims of the 'compassion traps'—the need to serve others and provide tenderness and compassion *at all times.*"[9] It is agreed that women are expected to provide tenderness and compassion, but not to do so when they are ill-treated or abused. Nor do we agree that they are expected to serve others altruistically. Service is to be provided by male or female when it is legitimate to those who deserve it, men or women.

Aggressiveness and rude reaction, in my view, is irrelevant to women's liberation. True liberation of the woman means her freedom to make decisions affecting herself, her freedom to choose her spouse, recognition of the woman as a legal person capable of conducting her own business, her feeling that she is

---

[8]Quoted in *Time Magazine* (May 19, 1975), p. 65, from Phelps and Nancy Austin's "The Assertive Woman"
[9]*Ibid.*

loved, respected and well-cared for. It does not mean breaking the code of decency, wearing revealing attire and behaving in a manner not in keeping with her dignity.

Coming now to the Muslim women's liberation movement, which, as has been observed, assumes a patient moderate course of persuasion rather than glamorous militancy, is, I believe, a healthy social phenomenon. Although its leadership is vested in the upper class, top female officials or spouses of top officials, which is true in some other Eastern countries, as demonstrated by the leadership of the delegations of these countries to the International Women's Conference held in Mexico City in 1975, the movement provides a healthy platform for women. It participates in public services, engages in welfare work, sets up welfare institutions, contributes to the education and training of women and organizes the efforts of women's consciousness-raising and stirs their awareness.

*　*　*

Let me now address myself to you, my sisters in faith and leaders of the feminist movements. Let not the dazzling glamour of the extremist elements in the Western liberation movements ever allure you. Listen not to those who claim that a sex revolution means a complete break with the past institutions and the elimination of all taboos and prohibitions. They are rejected at home by eminent female leaders. Although they condemn traditional stereotypes, they themselves behave in public according to the pattern which they criticize. Experiments in non-traditional marriages and family styles have badly failed. This is simply because the traditional styles are more workable and fulfilling. So let not the attribute "conservatism" bother you.

Please, sisters, seek to reach a full agreement with the agents of strict traditions. We do not need to abandon any details of the law of our faith when we seek to achieve healthy reforms in the interest of society. After all, the goal of religion is to guide us on the way to happiness and fulfillment on earth and in the Hereafter. We only need to seek an enlightened understanding of the law and reach reasonable interpretations.

And you, my American sisters. You have adopted Islam and chosen it as your faith. So let its teachings reform and tranform you. Seek deep satisfaction inside your soul by improving your relationship with your Lord through obedience to his law. Appear not in public unless your body is fully covered. You do not become more civilized or more beautiful by exposing more of your flesh. Respect your husband. Obey his wishes. Let him feel that he is the beloved and loved master of his castle under whose shelter you and your children are protected. Take good care of your children, and show them that you respect and obey their father; they will obey and respect him and will love you and respect you and will be better and well-adjusted characters of whom you will be proud. Remember that cleanliness, purity, grace, demureness, contentedness and self-respect are among the Muslim woman's virtues. It is true that we live in a country which does not profess to be following the Islamic law of marriage. Yet, we have to obey and respect its laws so long as they do not conflict with our religion; I mean so long as they do not deter us from carrying out our religious duties or compel us to commit a sin. This is the teaching of our religion. It is also in our own interest to respect these laws.

And you, my dear sisters who have come to America to join your dear husbands. Having been uprooted from your home climate, I know you have to go through a difficult period of adjustment, not only to the moods and habits of your husband but also to the American climate, a climate of great pressures and strains in spite of its liberalism and riches. Believe me these strains and pressures relate to your husband as they do to you. So please be patient and understanding. I know your husband may leave you alone at home to go to work, and you will miss the company of your family and your neighborhood at home. Please never feel lonely or bored. Anybody can feel lonely, if he wishes, even when he is in a crowded street, and can feel great even alone in a desert. That depends upon your mind. Seek to find a job or engage your mind in something useful. You always have God in your company. Inevitably your husband will see girls in the course of his work in his office, in his factory, in his clinic or wherever he happens to be. Be not overly jealous, and give not in to Satanic suspicions. Keep in good shape to please him and to attract him. If your heart labors under a heavy burden of evil thoughts, unfold it to your husband quietly and pleasantly. You will find him more sympathetic. He will shower great love upon you. Seek not to show off that you are progressive or a liberated woman by imitating manners or seeking glamour incompatible with your traditional values. It demeans you. Your liberation is in your mind.

CHAPTER VIII
THE UNITED NATIONS' REFORMS

Efforts and Documents:

The internationally increasing concern over the position of women in society is manifested in the tremendous efforts made by the United Nations toward the objective of improving the status of women throughout the world.

The United Nations is to be commended for its admirable work on behalf of women. Its concern over the position of women from the time of its inception led to the foundation of a special United Nations' commission on women as early as 1946. The United Nations' specialized agencies conducted valuable researches which have yielded massive useful data and led to enlightened recommendations that would in the most part benefit women and society at large. Such prodigious achievements could be performed by such a resourceful body whose goal is to serve humanity as such, unhindered by the limitations of a national policy or the consideration of parochial interests.

Women's rights are generally assured under the terms of the Charter of the United Nations as well as the Universal Declaration of Human Rights and other conventions and declarations issued by the World Organization and its agencies, particularly the ILO and the UNESCO, which are of universal application, promoting human equality and calling for the elimination of all types of prejudices and discrimination and are therefore beneficial to women. Besides these efforts, the United Nations issued instruments dealing with subjects of special interest to women and their status.

These include: a Convention on the Political Rights of Women, (1952), a Convention on the Nationality of Married Women, (1957), a Convention and Recommendations on Consent to Marriage, Minimum Age for Marriage and Registrations of Marriage (1962 and 1965), a Declaration on the Elimination of Discrimination against Women, (1967), a Program of Concerted International Action for the Advanment of Women, (1970), and a World Plan of Action, (1975). Although some governments and interested parties may be slow in complying with the call of these instruments, they expose the oppression of women, enhance their cause, define their rights and give them legitimacy where they are denied.

International Women's Year:

On December 18, 1972, the General Assembly of the United Nations resolved to proclaim 1975 as the International Women's Year. The aim of this proclamation was to focus attention on the plight of women in many parts of the world and create a better climate for accepting the reality of women's equality with men. The General Assembly urged that during the said year efforts should be intensified toward the fulfillment of the goal of equality, the promotion of women's integration in development action and the enhancement of their role in fostering world peace. Thus the theme of the IWY was threefold: Equality, Development and Peace.

In response to the call of the General Assembly a wide range of consciousness-raising activities including speeches, seminars, symposia and exhibitions took place during the IWY in many parts of the world. Some were sponsored by the United Nations itself, some by its various bodies, some by governments and by official or non-official organizations all over the world. Many governments established commissions on women in their own lands, and women's day was also observed in many parts of the world. Imaginative ideas were enunciated, relevant scientific literature containing significant revealing data was produced, and regional work programs for training women in various areas were inaugurated in Africa and Asia.

Although some feminist leaders do not feel that the International Women's Year was of much avail, and some even see it as a curse as they think that it has diverted efforts away from working for the ratification of the ERA, it is indeed too early to judge the value of the IWY so soon. During that year, the seeds were planted, and I strongly feel that the fruit will be born in the ensuing years. Success should not be measured in terms of isolated incidents, such as the election of a woman or the appointment of another to a high office, but rather by the degree of changes in attitude toward women's rights and their treatment.

The World Conference of the International Women's Year:

By far the most spectacular event during the IWY was the World Conference of Women sponsored by the United Nations which was held in Mexico City in the middle of that year (June 19-July 2, 1975). The Conference was the first of its kind ever to be held in history. It was also truly representative, as 133 governments were represented in it. There were also delegates from 10 intergovernmental and 113 non-governmental organizations, in addition to representatives from 8 liberation movements and 23 United Nations organs and specialized agencies. The total number of delegates was 1,221.

Since the conference was a governmental meeting from which persons with no official status were excluded, a parallel conference was held simultaneously in the same city, which provided a forum of discussion for experts on women's affairs and for the interested public. That forum was called The Tribune. At some points the excitement generated at the uninhibited Tribune, which drew the leading stars in the feminist movements, overshadowed the activities of the solemn yet colorful governmental conference.

The official conference which was opened by the President of Mexico and addressed by the United Nations' Secretary General and the United Nations' (lady) Commissioner on Women, as well as by the leading heads of governmental delegations, dealt with a large agenda, each item supported by documents and expert data. The most important item on the agenda was the World Plan of Action, which was the business of the first committee of the conference. This document which was adopted by the Conference with some minor additional amendments to its Introduction, was the best and major product of the whole activities of the IWY. It sums up the trends and thoughts of men and women in the United Nations who are the experts and the policy makers in the area of women's affairs. Much more will be said about it presently.

Apart from endorsing the World Plan of Action, the World Conference also adopted a statement which became known as the "Declaration of Mexico" and took a number of other resolutions. This Declaration reiterated the importance of the goal of equality of women and men, the woman's right to freedom and dignity, the right of individuals and couples to "decide freely and responsibly" the number and spacing of their children, and the need for fair distribution of wealth among nations, respect of national sovereignty and the need for international cooperation for peace and the role that could and should be played by women toward these objectives. In its own words, the Declaration emphatically acknowledges the women's "vital role in the promotion of peace in all spheres of life: in the family, the community, the nation and the world".

The 34 other decisions taken by the conference pertain to the status of women in various regions and include recommendations for the implementation of the World Plan of Action.

As for the Tribune, it was only meant as a platform for discussion, not for making recommendations. Undeterred by distance and traffic congestion, some of the radical feminists sought to lobby among the official delegates of the conference; and 15 members submitted proposals for amendments in the text of the World Plan of Action. These amendments mainly added emphasis to the meaning of the text.

Declaration on the Elimination of Discrimination Against Women:

It is not my aim to deal here with the voluminous work of the United Nations on behalf of women, but to make a few observations on some of the recommendations made in the Declaration on the Elimination of Discrimination Against Women, and in the World Plan of Action. These two documents can be regarded as the greatest landmarks in the action of the United Nations on behalf of women.

The Declaration, which was adopted by the General Assembly of the United Nations in November 1967, lays great emphasis on the idea of equality which is often encountered in most of its eleven articles. Its adoption needed great pressure, involving revisions and amendments in its text, as the Declaration faced stiff opposition by some delegates of the Third World countries who thought that some of its provisions conflicted with their traditions.

The Declaration urges measures to be taken by governments and responsible organizations that would insure fair play to women and lead to the removal of all kinds of prejudicial practices and customs. It recommends legislation to guarantee women equal chances in education and economics, and full participation in public life. All this is admirable and is consistent with our beliefs. My particular interest, however, is in Article 6 of the Declaration, which deals with the position of women in the family. Section 2 of this article stresses "the principle of equality of status of the husband and wife". Clause (b) of this section states that "Women shall have equal rights with men during marriage and at its dissolution", and clause (c) of the same section declares that "Parents shall have equal rights and duties in matters relating to their children".

Equality of the status of husband and the status of wife stressed in the Declaration apparently means the equality of rights and responsibilities emanating from them. It also seems to imply a denial of the need for domestic leadership as if leadership were incongruous with the concept of equality. The conjecture is sustained by clause (114), occurring in the Report of the Consultative Committee for the World Conferrence, (E/Conf. 66/BP/18) dated April 28, 1975, in which the concept of the head of the family is described as "outdated and discriminatory". This view can be easily refuted on anthropological, historical and organizational grounds.

It is our strong view that the domestic unit must have

leadership, and that the leadership should be vested in the male spouse. It is his responsibility to shield his spouse and provide for her. We believe this to be the equitable workable pattern. The husband can then exercise his manly qualities of determination and self-confidence with care and concern, patience, forbearance and forgiveness; and the wife, his equal and respectful companion, lends support, extends counsel to, and cooperates with her beloved partner. This pattern of reciprocal relationship, mutual love, cooperation and dedication is the natural style, consistent with the masculinity and femininity of the spouses, in which each party complements the other and which establishes a solid basis for efficiency and harmony. The status of the wife and the status of the husband are equally important, but are different with different reciprocal duties emanating from them. This is by no means inconsistent with the concept of equality in human dignity and in civil and legal rights.

The success and popularity among many American wives of the teachings of two recently propagated philosophies, "the Fascinating Womanhood" and "the Total Woman", which preach a complete submission and devotion by the wife to the service and happiness of her husband, lends support to the conjugal pattern of relationship we recommend and in which the wife's role is complementary to that of her husband. We do not recommend, however, such complete submission or subscribe to the details these schools prescribe to the wife in order that she would constantly seek to arrest her husband's attention and provoke his arousal. Their styles border on the verge of degrading inferiority for the woman and make her a constant slave to her sexual passion.

The Declaration's call for equal rights to women and men during marriage and at its dissolution is fair and unfair, and is therefore agreeable and disagreeable. Husband and wife have an equal right to be treated each by the other with dignity and respect. They should have equal right in deciding the continuation or seeking the dissolution of marriage. But the wife has special rights due to her from her husband during marriage and after its dissolution. To deprive her of these rights would be harsh and unfair. In marriage, she has a right to protection and maintenance from her husband, and after its dissolution she has a right to alimony and unless she is remarried or morally disqualified, to the custody of her children at least up to the age of seven for boys and the age of nine for girls. The wife owes her husband a right; namely, obedient regard for his leadership.

Again, to insist that parents shall have equal rights and duties in matters related to their children is similarly a double-edged sword. Parents are equally responsible for rearing their children and are to treat them with responsible love and concern. Yet their mother has greater rights and lesser legal burdens. The cost of their maintenance and education is the responsibility of their father, and the mother has greater moral duties upon her children.

This pattern sets a fair equilibrium compatible with sex differences and is by no means inimical to the sense of moral equality. What is important is not quantitative equality, but equity, domestic harmony, peace, love and stability.

The World Plan of Action:

The 45-page plan traces in its Introduction the roots of discrimination against women in elements ingrained in the socio-economic structure, especially of developing countries, and in the inequity in the distribution of the world income, two-thirds of which are captured by one-third of the world population. The Plan then sets out to propose actions that should be taken to remedy the situation on national, organizational, regional and international levels.

Apart from the Introduction, the Plan has six chapters on "National Action", "Specific Areas for National Action", "Research, Data Collection and Analysis", "Mass Communication Media", "International and Regional Action", and "Review and Appraisal". The policies recommended in the second chapter, which includes sections on the family, population, education, health, housing and other social questions, is of tremendous interest, although the recommendations in the other chapters are equally valuable.

The Plan, in Chapter VI, in order to enhance compliance

with its directives, urged that assessment of the progress toward the achievement of its goals should be made at reasonable intervals. This, in my opinion, will be useful in another direction. The investigation may reveal some points of weakness that may exist in the strategies of the Plan. It is relevant to recall here that the World Conference resolved to recommend that the period of ten years, 1975-1985 be proclaimed a "Decade of Women and Development", and that another world conference on women be convened in 1980 by the United Nations. These decisions, which were endorsed by the General Assembly, should stimulate sustained interest in the affairs of women during the decade; and results of investigations and recommendations that might be made in the light of assessment can be submitted to the proposed conference for action.

The World Plan of Action is a splendid document which offers illuminating guidelines both for national and international actions, especially where it deals with such specific areas as education, employment and health and nutrition. Admirable are its words occurring in clause 112 under the section on the Family, which read:

> "Household activities which are necessary for family life
> have generally been perceived as having a low economic
> and social prestige. All societies, should, however, place
> a higher value on these activities if they wish the family
> group to be maintained and to fulfill its basic functions
> of the procreation and education of the children."

I am also fascinated by the theme of domestic dynamism observed in article 111 of the Plan, and the call for the preservation of human dignity under all conditions which are both acknowledged and provided for under the law of Islam pertaining to the roles of the spouses. By a role here I mean the function, the part played by a spouse for the wellbeing of the social unit, the family. It is a role of reciprocal attitudes and cooperation, not a rigid distribution of the particular items of housework. It is the pattern of attitude to be assumed by each party toward the other, generated by the mode of relationship advocated by Islam. According to this complementary pattern, the role of the husband is not subjugation or authoritarian domination, but provision, protection, pardoning, generosity and loving concern. That of the wife is cooperation, decision-sharing, gentleness, domestic cohesion, tender love, devotion, elimination of tension and the satisfaction of the emotional needs.

The World Plan of Action, which is couched in careful terms, is somewhat silent on the subject of the necessity of the institution of the family, which we regard not only as the basic indispensable unit of society but also the prototype of all human organizations and grouping, including the state itself. Neither does the Plan categorically call for equal rights and responsibilities between married couples, although it does so implicitly in clause 117. The Declaration of Mexico is more categorical on that.

We do not agree to interpret equality in the sense of sameness, but in the sense that the mutual rights and responsibilities of the spouses are equally important and equally valuable. They have much in common but diverge, just as much as male and female are essentially similar but different not only genetically but also intellectually and behaviorally. Intellectual differences are slight, but research has found that most girls cluster close to the average whereas boys widely diverge at both ends. Behaviorally, boys tend to be more aggressive and more ambitious, and girls are more nurturing and more dependable. These differences are reflected in the boys' greater skill in mathematical and mechanical tasks. Their interest is generally more object-oriented. The girls' interests are generally more people-oriented. They are more skilled linguistically and in subtle manual works. When organizational expansion increasingly grew, the demure woman, occupied in her patient, time-comsuming traditional domestic tasks hesitated to, or was compelled not to move forward with the time to diversify her activities and compete with men at all levels. She stayed at home, and the object-oriented male had a monopoly on public work.

Women's liberation, in a sense, lies in their overcoming this complex, and the removal of obstacles created by men from the way of the woman seeking to fulfill her aspirations.

In spite of our fascination with the World Plan of Action, one does not feel comfortable with its clauses 114 and 120, where it seems to condone moral laxity when it insists on legislations to protect the "rights" of women involved in "consensual union" and on granting full-fledged status of a parent to unwed mothers and extending the same rights and obligations of children born in wedlock to children born out of wedlock. It is good to be charitable even to sinners, but it is unfair to equate perpetual sinners with virtuous people, or the consequences of sin with the fruit of virtue. To do so is to encourage the pursuit of immorality. The large increase in the number of so called "unwed mothers" and of the incidence of childbirth out of wedlock does not alter the moral character of the act leading to these phenomena. Compliance with such recommendations, I fear, would reduce the value of marriage and might open the door to greater corruption and abuses.

The World Plan of Action also lays emphasis on family planning and on educating women in the use of its methods. Hopefully, the authors of the Plan do not mean to include resort to abortion as one of the measures, especially when a pregnancy is in an advanced stage. I also hope that the training in the use of contraceptives so strongly recommended is only meant for married persons and couples contemplating marriage. To make it available for unmarried youngsters unaccompanied by restraining moral training would be like giving an untrained youth a highly powered motor car without a brake.

The above observations do not by any means scale down our appreciation of the great services rendered by the United Nations to humanity, nor do we ever underestimate its immense achievements in the areas related to the status of women. We only hope that the World Organization, which commands our great esteem and in which we have placed our trust, shall always, when it makes universal recommendations, take greater consideration of the people's deeply-rooted traditions and values especially when they are so sensible and equitable. The experience of the Nordic nations may not be of the same value to African and Asian nations. People's needs, temperaments and values vary widely. Moreover, greater emphasis should be laid upon education rather than formal legislation. Compliance generated by the fear of the law is of lower value than a virtue cultivated and nourished by greater knowledge.

SUMMING UP

Living things perpetuate themselves through the process of reproduction. Survival is the ultimate purpose of their behavioral activities. Nature takes care of the reproductive process in the case of the world of plants. The animal kingdoms initiate the process instinctively.

Survival of the human species, which is endowed with intellect and is living for a moral mission, unlike the botanical and the zoological survival which is merely biological, has cultural and moral contents and can only blossom within the bond of marriage and the institution of the family.

Success of these institutions which are instrumental to human biological, cultural and moral survival depends, in the first place, on their protection from disruptive anti-marital, pre-marital and extra-marital activities. In the second place, the relationship between the male and the female categories of the species has to be built on the mutual recognition of their birthright to dignity and respect, and the fulfillment of their similar or reciprocal roles in society based upon the realities of their equality and differences.

The irony is that the party who bears the greater burden in human reproduction and nurturing, the gentle half of humanity who deserves to be adored and revered, has been denied equal rights and subjected to oppression and discrimination sustained by harsh mythology and legal solemnity. The struggle by the feminists should not therefore be summarily resented or indiscriminately resisted. Yet, the feminist leadership, in defining its goals, should endeavor to restore the women's rights on the basis of equity and with imaginative magnanimity, permitting no reaction to past prejudices to push it on the side of forces which are seeking to legitimatize practices that encroach upon the sanctity of human life and are inimical to cherished moral values.

Lastly, the family, in order to fulfil its noble function, needs an atmosphere of peace and harmony. This in turn depends upon the couple's ability to adjust, to accommodate and compromise. Their ability can be greatly enhanced by their belief in the Creator, their awareness of His constant presence and their deep commitment to serve Him through compliance with His divine law. This commitment makes life more meaningful and helps them in their endeavor to adjust and in their pursuit of happiness. Their goal in life is neither exclusively spiritual nor merely materialistic. It partakes of both. In their pursuit of joy and pleasure they believe to be fulfilling a divine guidance. When they attain pleasure or success, they feel thankful to God. Attainment of success is not merely the fruit of their efforts, but a favor and a gift from their Lord. Their joy is generated not merely by their earthly sensations but also by their anticipation of divine rewards.

To wise men and women, the desire to attain God's pleasure is the central focal point, always present in their mind. Everything else—pleasure derived from marriage, joy of having children, job success, popularity with others, as well as failure, pain, stresses, crises, and all—are peripheral phenomena. Earthly life is a journey leading to a more worthy and a more lasting life. When a believer travels in fair weather or in storms, he knows his journey is but a passage to a coveted destination. Conscious of his worthy goal and less sensitive to worldly failures, he neither despairs nor seeks outlets in unethical practices. He learns how to integrate his crises and lets them not reflect on his relations with others, particularly his life partner. His conscience is his counsellor, and his faith is his therapy.

EPILOGUE

At last a book that clears up our misconceptions concerning the role of women in Islam! Dr. Muhammad Abdul-Rauf, an authority on the Koran and the Hadiths of the Prophet Muhammad, peace be upon him, has spent many careful hours outlining for us the roles of Muslim women as wives, mothers, job holders, and as members of society at large. What makes this a special book is that it is not merely Dr. Abdul-Rauf's own reflections about women's rights, but it is an explanation of the Koranic teachings concerning this matter. The author goes to the source—the Word of God as written in the Koran, and it is with this authority that he speaks. Lest anyone feel that his book is the last word on the subject, let us assure him that it is only the beginning of a research project that should be conducted by women and men interested in the progress of women today.

The Women of the Muslim community are indeed grateful for a book which states so clearly our rights. Immediately, Dr. Abdul-Rauf establishes that women under Islam are equal to men in the sight of God. This eliminates the false conception of some non-Muslims that Muslim women have been assigned an inferior status. To the contrary, Muslim women are highly respected. They are equal under the Islamic law. If a Muslim woman does the same job as a man she must be paid an equivalent salary. If a woman earns her own money, though she be married, she is entitled to keep it, unless she chooses to do otherwise. This concept of equality holds true in every aspect of Muslim life.

The author takes time to explain the reason behind the feminine style of dress promoted by Islam. Among us Westerners, it seems to be a fairly common misconception that Muslim women cover their bodies out of a feeling of shame. On the contrary, I have discovered, Muslim women are extremely proud of that which God gave them. In their modesty they find dignity. They save their beauty only for those who actually care for them—their parents and their husband—rather than entice each passerby. The Muslim woman knows there is nothing honorable about making herself available to just anyone who may look her way. She respects herself and on this account she covers herself.

A large part of Dr. Abdul-Rauf's book is given to reestablishing the importance of building strong marriages—for our children's sake and for the sake of society. First, if our marriages are to last, they must be God-centered. Only then will we treat one another with true love and fairness. Then we will help each other—doing what we can to work as a harmonious unit. We even have the example of the Prophet Muhammad and his wives. They loved him and served him and so he did the same. One of the most vivid examples we have is that of the Prophet Muhammad tending the children, cooking, and sewing his own clothes—even with the heavy responsibility of leader of his people. Islam is a practical religion in which concrete examples of good and proper behavior are set down. Surely such an example set by the Prophet and his wives should encourage men to help their wives, and wives to help their husbands.

Finally the book looks at the changing role of women throughout the world. It makes note of the progress being made in America toward establishing the equality of women, and compares it with European and African society. That progress may not be the same everywhere but a book like Dr. Abdul-Rauf's should indicate to us that the first steps toward true equality for women were made by Islam. Fourteen hundred years ago, before the advent of Islam, women were looked upon as the lowest of the low. Only Islam raised them up to their position of true equality with men. This is a tradition we as Muslims must understand and maintain. Again, thanks to the author who has begun the process of enlightenment for all those of the Muslim Community.

Diana Eleanora Cerruti
Alexandria, Virginia

BIBLIOGRAPHY

A. *Koran and Hadith*

The Koran, (References are to the standard well-known Egyptian edition.)

Hadith: The following classical compilations:

    Abu Dawud, Sulayman Ibn al-Ash'ath, *Sunan,* Beirut Reproduction, n.d., (4 volumes).

    Bukhari, al-, Muhammad Ibn Ismail, *Sahih,* Halabi Press, Cairo, 1953, (4 volumes).

    Ibn Hanbal, Ahmad, *al-Musnad,* Beirut Reproduction of Cairo Edition, 1313 A.H. (6 volumes).

    Ibn Majah, Abu 'Abd Allah, Muhammad Ibn Yazid, *Sunan,* Halabi Press, Cairo, 1953, (2 volumes).

    Malik Ibn Anas, *al-Muwatta',* Sha'b Press, Cairo, 1951.

    Muslim Ibn Hajjaj, *Sahih,* Halabi Press, Cairo, n.d., (2 volumes).

    Nasa'i, al-, *Sunan,* Misriyyah Press, Cairo, 1930. (Accompanied by Sayuti's Commentary, 8 volumes).

    Shaikh Ala 'ud-Din, *Kanz ul-'Ummal,* (Haydarabad, 1312 A.H.)

    Tirmidhi, al-, Muhammad 'Abd Al-Rahman, *Jami',* Madani Press, Cairo, 1963, (10 volumes).

B. *Works*

Abdul Rauf, Muhammad, *Islam: Faith and Devotion,* Islamic Publication Bureau, Lagos, Nigeria, 1974.

    Life and Teaching of the Prophet Muhammad, Longmans, Green and Co., Ltd., 1964. Reprinted in 1975.

Abu A'la Maududi, *Purdah and the Status of Women in Islam,* Islamic Publications Ltd., Lahore, 1972.

Alexander, William, *History of Women and their Treatment in All Ages,* 1835.

Amin, Qasim, *Tahir al-Mar'ah,* (Woman's Liberation), Cairo, 1970.

Al-'Aqqad, 'Abbass Mahmud, *al-Mar'ah fi al-Qur'an,* Women in the Koran), Cairo, 1971.

Birri-al, Zakariyya, *al-Ahkam al-Asasiyyah li-al-Usrah al-Islamiyyah,* (The Basic Rules for the Muslim Family), Ittihad al-'Arabi Press, Cairo, 1974.

Draz, M. Abdullah, *La Morale du Koran,* Paris, Presses Universitaires de France, 1951.

Ghazzali, Muhammad, nicknamed Abu Hamid, *Ihya' 'Ulum al-Din,* (Revival of the Sciences of Religion), Cairo, 1933.

Guillaume, Alfred, *The Life of Muhammad,* Oxford University Press, 1955.

Gibb, Hamilton A. R. and H. Bowen, *Islamic Society and the West,* London, Oxford University Press, 1957.

Gildre, George F., *Sexual Suicide,* Bantam Books, U.S.A., 1973.

Juzayri-al, 'Abd al-Rahman, *al-Fiqh 'ala al-Madhahib al-Arba'ah,* (The Islamic Law According to the Four Legal Schools), Vol. IV, Tujariyyah Press, Cairo, n.d.

Kharufah, 'Ala al-Din, *Sharh Qanum al-Ahwal al-Shakhsiyyah,* (Commentary on the Law of Personal Status), Baghdad, 1962.

Nafsawi, al, Shaikh 'Umar Ibn Muhammad, *The Perfumed Garden,* Translated by Sir Richard Burton, Paris, 1964.

Rasheed, Bahija Sidqy, *The Egyptian Feminist Union,* Cairo, The Anglo-Egyptian Bookshop, 1973.

Siddiqi, Muhammad Mazheruddin, *Women in Islam,* Lahore, The Institute of Islamic Culture, 1959.

Stein, Gertrude H., *Marriage in Early Islam,* The Royal Asiatic Society, 1939.

United Nations
  (a) *Declaration on the Elimination of Discrimination Against Women,* Litho in U.N., N.Y., (OPI/297), November 1973-20M.
  (b) *The Interaction of Women in the Development Process as Equal Partners with Men,* (E/Conf. 66/4), 1975.
  (c) i -*World Plan of Action,* (E/Conf. 66/5), 1975.
     ii-*"Review and Appraisal of Progress Made to Implement the Goals of the International Development Strategy and of General Assembly Resolution (XXV),"* E/CN-6/598, 21 July 1976.

Wafi, 'Ali 'Abd al-Wahid, *al-Mar'ah fi al-Islam,* (Women in Islam), Cairo, Maktabat Gharib, 1971.

The Women's Organisation of Iran, *The Iranian Woman, Past and Present,* Tehran, 1976.

Woodsmall, Ruth Frances, *Moslem Women Enter a New World,* Round Table Press, Inc., New York, 1936 and 1960, Ed. by The Middle East Institute, Washington, D.C.